Christianity, Cults, and World Religions

A Bible Class Course for Adults

Roland Cap Ehlke

NORTHWESTERN PUBLISHING HOUSE
Milwaukee, Wisconsin

Picture credits: p. 10, Clif Koeller; p. 17, Utah State Historical Society; p. 22, Northwestern Publishing House; p. 27, Library of Congress; p. 35, Unification Church; p. 40, R. C. Ehlke; p. 46, *The Baha'i Faith;* p. 47, Baha'i Office of Public Information; p. 52, R. C. Ehlke; p. 58, Jerry Koser; p. 66, Northwestern Publishing House; p. 67, clip art; p. 73, Concordia Publishing House; p. 78, clip art.

Cover design: Kurt Adams and R. C. Ehlke

Fourth printing, 1999
Third printing, 1996
Second printing, 1993

All Scripture quotations, unless otherwise indicated, are taken from the HOLY BIBLE, NEW INTERNATIONAL VERSION®. NIV®. Copyright © 1973, 1978, 1984 by International Bible Society. Used by permission of Zondervan Publishing House. All rights reserved.

The "NIV" and "New International Version" trademarks are registered in the United States Patent and Trademark Office by International Bible Society. Use of either trademark requires the permission of International Bible Society.

All rights reserved. No part of this publication may be reproduced, stored in a retrieval system, or transmitted in any form or by any means—electronic, mechanical, photocopying, recording, or otherwise—except for brief quotations in reviews, without prior permission from the publisher.

Northwestern Publishing House
1250 N. 113th St., Milwaukee, WI 53226-3284
© 1992 by Northwestern Publishing House.
Published 1992
Printed in the United States of America
ISBN 0-8100-0438-0

*Dedicated
to
Dianne*

Contents

	Introduction	7
1.	Modern Religious Pluralism	9
2.	Mormonism	14
3.	Jehovah's Witnesses	20
4.	Christian Science	26
5.	The Unification Church	32
6.	The Muslims	38
7.	Baha'i	45
8.	Hinduism	51
9.	The New Age Movement	57
10.	Astrology	65
11.	Satanism	71
12.	Christ Crucified Is the Key	77

Introduction

As we near the close of the second millennium after our Savior's birth, we are confronted with a bewildering array of religions challenging Christianity. As never before, we need to "contend for the faith that was once for all entrusted to the saints" (Jude 3).

This means, above all, that Christians are to be well-grounded in biblical truth. But it also means that we ought to have some acquaintance with the beliefs of others around us and how those beliefs differ from what the Bible teaches. This will enable us better to share our faith as opportunity presents itself. It also helps us appreciate just how brilliantly unique the Christian faith is.

Only biblical Christianity offers a Savior, rather than another set of rules for trying to save ourselves. Only biblical Christianity offers Jesus Christ!

Those using this book for a Bible study class are urged to read the lessons at home before attending class. In class, review the lesson and discuss whatever questions came to mind in home reading. The questions following each lesson offer ideas to stimulate class participation.

The course allows for a great deal of flexibility. A Bible study group need not examine all twelve topics. For example, your church might choose to offer a five week course focusing on American-grown religions. This would mean using the introductory lesson and conclusion, as well as the lessons on the Mormons, Jehovah's Witnesses, and Christian Science (lessons 1,2,3,4,12). Or you may decide on a six week course concentrating on major world religions and their spin-offs: Islam,

Baha'ism, Hinduism, the New Age (1,6,7,8,9,12). In each case, it's advisable to include the introductory and concluding lessons, because of the overviews they offer.

With the exception of the lesson on the New Age, the basics of this Bible study course first appeared as a series of articles in the *Northwestern Lutheran* from 1990 to 1991. There is much turmoil in today's religious scene, and with the passing of time, changes are constantly taking place. Yet the main tenets of religions aren't going to change. Leaders of course will. So will membership statistics.

Although they will become somewhat dated, we are supplying statistics (current at the time of publication). This gives an idea of the relative size of the various groups. As time goes by, it might be helpful to find the latest statistics on each group. This will give an indication as to whether or not the group under discussion has been flourishing in recent years. Useful sources for such updates are *The World Almanac and Book of Facts* (New York: Pharos Books, published yearly); *Yearbook of American and Canadian Churches* (Nashville: Abingdon Press, published yearly); *Handbook of Denominations* (Nashville: Abingdon Press, now in its ninth edition).

Each lesson suggests two or three books for further reading on the topic. Some of these are specific to one cult or religion; others are general. If you need to limit your additional sources, we suggest *The Kingdom of the Cults* by Walter Martin (Minneapolis: Bethany, 1985) and the "Response Series," a set of booklets covering a wide range of religions (St. Louis: Concordia).

The lessons also include illustrations and a quick reference, "Fingertip facts," to help clarify distinctive elements of the various religions. For those using the video that accompanies this Bible study, we suggest showing the ten-minute segment for each lesson as an introduction or discussion starter at the beginning of class.

We offer this study with the prayer that it will increase your appreciation for the uniqueness and pricelessness of the Christian faith. May it also enable you better to contend for that faith and share it with others.

1. Modern Religious Pluralism

> *Time:* An evening in April, the early 1990s.
> *Place:* A small, out-of-the-way conference room in a large Midwestern university student union.
> *Occasion:* A handful of people—ten to be exact—has gathered for the meeting of a self-titled "new age" religious group.
> *The meeting:* A soft-spoken woman, who introduces herself as Patty, opens the meeting with a brief welcome. The room is then darkened for a twenty-minute video, which presents numerous personal testimonials of people who claim to have undergone out-of-the-body experiences and soul travel. The video includes a message from the Living Spiritual Master to his devotees, "We are moving into a golden age...."
> When the video is done, the group joins in chanting, "HU ... HU-U-U. ..." This "ancient name for God" is chanted six times; then there is silence. After that the people share their personal spiritual experiences.

This little scene probably strikes us as rather strange or exotic. It may also strike us as insignificant. The vast majority of people on that campus had overlooked notices of the meeting. Apparently they could not have cared less what went on there.

Yet this scenario takes place countless times each week across our land. It is a microcosm of the huge religious upheaval taking place today. Indeed, all of the Western world, once considered the stronghold of Christendom, is in spiritual upheaval.

Upheaval

According to the *World Christian Encyclopedia* (David B. Barrett, ed. Nairobi; New York: Oxford University Press, 1982), Christian churches in Europe and North America are losing members at the astounding rate of 7600 each day! Here are some examples of mainline Christian church membership in America during the 1970s and 1980s:

	1971	**1980**	**1992**
United Church of Christ	1,858,592	1,740,202	1,625,969
United Methodist Church	10,036,109	9,534,803	8,979,139
Presbyterian Church	2,906,147	2,468,215	2,886,482

These figures represent a loss of 1,057,628 members from three church bodies in one decade (1971-1980). The Presbyterians did manage to gain during the next dozen years, but only through mergers with existing church bodies. The other two continued their slide, the Church of Christ losing another 114,233, and the Methodists 555,664.

Most Lutheran church bodies are also declining in membership. (Although the Wisconsin Synod managed to grow during the seventies, the eighties saw that growth come to a standstill. The synod's 3.6 percent growth during that decade marks the lowest for any decade in its history.)

Where are all the members going? Many have turned to charismatic, Pentecostal groups. The fastest growing of these is the As-

For many people today, mainline Christian churches are little more than relics of a bygone era.

semblies of God, which has shot up from about 300,000 members in 1971 to 2,160,667 in 1989. (Even this church dipped slightly in recent years, to 2,137,890 in 1992.)

New Christian denominations, sometimes referred to as sects, are on the rise. But that's only part of the picture. There is also a tremendous increase in groups outside the pale of Christianity. Established world religions, such as Hinduism and Islam, are making headway in the West. The same holds true for newer non-Christian cults, such as Mormonism and Baha'ism.

Religious researchers estimate there are as many as 2000 new religions in America. Clearly, ours is a society of religious pluralism.

The decline of mainline Christianity and rise of non-Christian religions have great impact on us and our children. No longer can we assume that most people accept basic Christian morality and teachings. No longer can churches rest on their laurels. Christianity is still the dominant religion in America, but the competition from other faiths is getting tougher.

Causes

What's behind this upheaval? As with any spiritual turmoil, at the root is Satan together with his legions. "For our struggle is not against flesh and blood," writes Paul, "but against the rulers, against the authorities, against the powers of this dark world and against the spiritual forces of evil in the heavenly realms" (Ephesians 6:12).

The devil has used a number of powerful forces in the modern world to weaken Christian churches and their proclamation, as well as to strengthen the inroads of anti-Christian groups. Two of those forces are humanism (the exaltation of man in place of God) and materialism (the exaltation of things in place of God). The media provide an almost steady stream of these two isms.

Yet the main damage to the churches has come not from without but from within. Many contemporary Christian denominations have sold their birthright for a mess of pottage.

In one area after another the churches have sold out to rationalism, placing human reason above God's revelation and the supernatural. From the special creation and flood of Genesis, to the Old Testament prophecies, to the miracles and resurrection of Jesus, to the heavenly vision of Revelation—theologians have denied God's power and wisdom. They have taken an inerrant, authoritative, and divinely inspired Bible and made it for themselves an error-ridden, powerless, and merely human book.

Having discarded the Bible, much of mainline Christianity has little left to offer except subjective advice. What a far cry from the gospel Jesus entrusted to his church—the good news of a Savior victorious over sin, death, Satan, and hell itself!

Secular forces and the weakness of the churches have combined to create a spiritual wasteland. People are hungering for spiritual food. Many are offering to satisfy that hunger.

Our role

While false religions from Armstrongism to Zen have been quick to capitalize on the present situation, orthodox Christians often have been sluggish to react. Could it be we've become too wearied from the doctrinal infighting among Christian denominations? Or have we been overly influenced by the world?

Until the end of time this world will remain a spiritual battlefield. We need to be aware of the dangers out there. Then, grounded solidly in God's word, we need to "contend for the faith" (Jude 3) and in love confess Christ to others.

In the next lessons we shall look at a number of cults and non-Christian religions which have made their presence felt among us. We shall see how they differ from the Bible and examine ways to share our Christian faith.

Further reading:

Beaver, R. Pierce, et al. *Eerdmans' Handbook to the World's Religions.* Grand Rapids: Wm. B. Eerdmans, 1982.

Jackson, Gregory L. *Liberalism: Its Cause and Cure.* Milwaukee: Northwestern, 1991.

Martin, Walter. *The Kingdom of the Cults.* Minneapolis: Bethany House, 1985.

For study and discussion:

1. Discuss various reasons why mainline Christian churches are often losing members or barely holding their own. To what

degree is it the churches' fault? To what degree is it because of the times in which we live?

2. Discuss Gamaliel's argument concerning the early Christians: "If their purpose or activity is of human origin, it will fail. But if it is from God, you will not be able to stop these men; you will only find yourselves fighting against God" (see Acts 5:27-40). Is the growth of a church body necessarily a sign that God is behind it? Give examples.

3. At times true religion can seem to fail outwardly. Think of the history of the Prophet Elijah (see 1 Kings 19:14-18). How did the Lord answer the discouraged prophet? How does God answer discouraged believers today?

4. How does the religious pluralism of today's society affect people's attitudes toward other religions? Do people tend to get confused? Do they give up trying to find out the differences? Is there a tendency toward acceptance, indifference, minimizing differences, not getting into religious discussions, and the like?

5. Discuss the inroads that humanism and materialism have made on modern life. Think of examples from daily life out in the world as well as church life.

6. Amid the turmoil of the twentieth century, what signs do we see that we are living in the end times? See Mark 13.

7. What are we doing to proclaim the gospel through our congregation or church body, and what more might we be doing?

2.
Mormonism

*A*mericans love a success story. And few rags to riches stories can match the rise of the Mormon Church, also known as the Church of Jesus Christ of Latter-Day Saints (LDS). This homegrown religion is multiplying by huge leaps. The LDS church's *daily* income is $4 million (1987 figure). And thanks to a highly successful media campaign, the church projects an image of almost perfect, clean-living families and freshly scrubbed, dedicated young missionaries in white shirts and black ties.

Mormon growth

Few, if any, American-based churches even come close to the accelerated growth of the LDS church. Every day two new chapels go up somewhere in the world and every two minutes one new member is baptized.

Founded in 1830, it took the church 117 years to reach one million members (1947). In the 45 years since then, the church has grown to seven million. The following figures represent the largest Mormon group, based in Salt Lake City. They are enough to make any evangelism-minded church member drool:

Year	Membership
1949	1.08 million
1959	1.62 million
1969	2.81 million
1979	4.40 million
1989	7.00 million

Over 40,000 Mormon missionaries carry their gospel to more than 50 countries worldwide. Young Mormons dedicate two years to such activities; older Mormon couples give three years.

(The Mormon missionary force is 79 percent young men; 13 percent young women; 8 percent couples.)

While some Mormon growth comes from such activities, a few other facts help put this in perspective. In recent years Mormon growth in the U.S. has slowed, thanks in part to a deluge of Bible-based, Christian material exposing the true nature of Mormonism. It now takes more man-hours, money, and PR for each new American convert. Only about one in a thousand knocks at the door results in a conversion.

Yet the church continues to expand through rapid overseas growth and through "obstetrical evangelism." Mormons are known for their large families, surpassing Roman Catholics in the average number of children.

Mormonism gains converts best where its true nature is least known. Although it often comes across as another Christian denomination, the LDS church is really a pagan cult. This may be one reason that Mormon missionaries don't discuss some of the unique doctrines of their religion until after numerous visits.

LDS teachings and practices

Beneath the clean-cut, all-American exterior of Mormonism lies a satanic set of doctrines. A few examples make this clear.

According to Mormon teaching, Jesus and Lucifer (Satan) were brothers, sons of God the Father and his wife, who live on a planet near a star named Kolob. Mormons consider the three Persons of the Trinity to be three separate gods among many other gods.

Joseph Smith, the founder of Mormonism, taught that "God himself was once as we are now and is an exalted man, who sits enthroned in yonder heavens!" Mormon doctrine goes on to explain that man can "inherit thrones, kingdoms, principalities, powers, and dominions." This doctrine of "eternal progression" asserts that people can progress to become gods, just like Jesus.

A well-known practice of the Mormons is baptism for the dead. They believe that people can become Mormons after death. Consequently, they have vicarious baptisms in the Mormon church for those who have already died. Interestingly, Martin Luther was baptized into the LDS church on October 10, 1922.

The Mormons have many other doctrines and practices that run counter to the Bible. One of the key LDS concepts is that of perfection. According to Pastor Mark Cares, who has worked extensively among Mormons, "the hub of their message" is that we are to strive for perfection. Viewing men and women as gods in embryo, and having a weak concept of sin, Mormonism looks at perfection as a heavy but manageable burden. Toward this end, good Mormons give a tenth of their income to the church and abstain from tea, coffee, tobacco, and liquor.

This striving for perfection, coupled with their missionary zeal, leads to many "stressed-out Mormons," says Cares. What Mormons lack is a Savior who brings the refreshing message that "it is by grace you have been saved, through faith . . . not by works" (Ephesians 2:8,9).

Joseph Smith and Brigham Young

Mormonism can be traced back to rather humble beginnings. In 1823 in Palmyra, New York, a seventeen-year-old lad by the name of Joseph Smith, Jr. was praying and supposedly had a vision of an angel called Moroni. The angel told Smith that he would find some sacred writings buried in a hill near Palmyra. It was not until several years later that Smith was able to get the sacred tablets and translate them. He said that the tablets were gold, that the writing was in "reformed Egyptian," and that he was able to decipher the writing by means of a pair of golden spectacles called "Urim and Thummim."

No one else saw the plates and no Egyptian scholar has ever heard of "reformed Egyptian." Nevertheless, Smith was a powerful individual and immediately had a following for his new religion. After his "translation" of the *Book of Mormon,* Smith said he gave the golden plates back to the angel.

The Mormons moved west from New York because of opposition to their growing church. They moved to Ohio, then to Independence, Missouri, and from there to Nauvoo, Illinois. Because of opposition from a newspaper, Smith and the Mormons ransacked and burned the newspaper office. After this incident Joseph Smith and his brother Hyrum were placed in a jail in Carthage, Illinois. There they were attacked and murdered by an angry mob in 1844.

The *Book of Mormon,* together with Smith's other writings, *Doctrine and Covenants* and *Pearl of Great Price,* remains on a level with the Bible as part of LDS scriptures. Most Mormons, however, rely more heavily on the words of the current church

Mormon Temple, Salt Lake City, Utah

leader and present-day publications, such as the periodical the *Ensign*.

Following Smith's martyrdom, most Mormons accepted the leadership of Brigham Young. It was Young who led the group to Utah in the late 1840s. There they set up a theocratic state which they saw as the establishment of the kingdom of God on earth. Like Smith, Young was a polygamist. Young, who had 25 wives, contended, "Jesus Christ was a polygamist; Mary and Martha, the sisters of Lazarus, were his plural wives, and Mary Magdalene was another. . . ."

Mormons who did not accept Young's leadership remained in Missouri. Today, the Reorganized Church of Jesus Christ of Latter-Day Saints numbers about ¼ million members and has its headquarters in Independence, Missouri. Other smaller Mormon splinter groups may be found in Missouri and scattered throughout the western states, especially Utah.

Reaching the Mormons

Most Christian efforts vis-a-vis the Mormons take one of two avenues: (1) they point to contradictions between LDS doctrine and the Bible; (2) they focus on the "skeletons in the closet" of early Mormon history (and there are many). Such approaches serve a useful purpose. Since much of Mormonism's growth comes from Protestant ranks, the dissemination of this information serves a defensive purpose. But it also tends to put Mormonism on the defensive and shuts off valuable communication.

Some, like Mark Cares, feel it is better to offer a positive witness, namely, the gospel of Jesus Christ. Burdened with their legalistic system, Mormons need to hear the invitation of Jesus, "Come to me, all you who are weary and burdened, and I will give you rest" (Matthew 11:28).

Although they have their repertory of Bible passages, most Mormon missionaries really don't know about the good news of salvation through Christ Jesus. In him we have the perfection we can never attain by our own efforts (Hebrews 10:10-14).

Many of these young people are also lonely and discouraged. Rather than a mere, "I'm not interested," might we not offer some friendship coupled with the witness of what Jesus means to us? The love of Christ is a success story we're a part of and we can share with others.

Fingertip facts:

Founding: 1830 in Fayette, New York, by Joseph Smith.
Authority: The *Book of Mormon* and other writings of J. Smith; pronouncements of church hierarchy.
Key teachings: Eternal progression; perfectionism.
View of the Bible: Paid lip service, but Mormon scriptures take precedence.
View of Jesus: A man, born of Adam and Mary, who progressed to godhead.
View of the Trinity: Three gods among many; God is not a spirit, but of material substance.
Salvation: Christ's death brought release from the grave; beyond this, salvation is by works; everyone will reach one of three levels of heaven.

Further reading:

Ball, John. *Saints of Another God.* Milwaukee: Northwestern, 1989.

Decker, Ed, and Dave Hunt. *The Godmakers* (also available on video). Eugene, OR: Harvest House, 1984.

For study and discussion:

1. Discuss the key points at which Mormonism differs from the Bible.

2. How does the Mormon teaching of celestial marriages (marriages last forever) differ with Matthew 22:23-33?

3. Success breeds success. How can the phenomenal growth of Mormons encourage members of that church? How does it impress outsiders?

4. What might Mormonism's slowed growth rate in the United States indicate?

5. Archaeology does not prove the Bible true in the sense that we base our faith on archaeological findings. Yet it often confirms what Scripture teaches. Why can archaeology not confirm history as related in the *Book of Mormon*?

6. At times Mormon doctrine contradicts Mormon scriptures. For example, the *Book of Mormon* teaches there is one God (Alma 11:26-29) and that he is triune: " . . . of the Father, and of the Son, and of the Holy Spirit, which is one God, without end" (2 Nephi 32:21). Yet Mormon doctrine teaches that there are many gods: "Three separate Personages—Father, Son, and Holy Ghost—comprise the Godhead. As each of these persons is a God, it is evident, from this standpoint alone, that a plurality of Gods exists. To us, speaking in the proper finite sense, these three are the only Gods we worship. But in addition there is an infinite number of holy personages, drawn from worlds without number, who have passed on to exaltation and are thus gods" (Bruce R. McConkie. *Mormon Doctrine.* Salt Lake City: Bookcraft, 1978). What might such discrepancies within the religion say about Mormonism?

7. Mormonism teaches that we are progressing toward becoming gods and that we do so by our own efforts. Compare this with what the Bible says. See Romans 5:12-19; Ephesians 2:1-10.

3. Jehovah's Witnesses

In many ways the Jehovah's Witness church is a reflection of Mormonism. Both are American born. Both were begun in the nineteenth century by dynamic, self-styled religious innovators—the Mormons by Joseph Smith, the Witnesses by Charles Taze Russell. These founders were succeeded by equally powerful men, Brigham Young and Joseph Franklin Rutherford. Both groups claim to be Christian, when in reality they are cults which deny the very basics of Christianity. Both are active in door-to-door witnessing and try to project a clean-cut, family-oriented image. Both have gained worldwide influence.

In some ways, however, the Jehovah's Witness organization has had to play second fiddle to its counterpart. The Witnesses, officially known as the Watchtower and Tract Society, got off to a later start (1879 vs. 1830). Although the Witnesses have enjoyed spectacular growth (3.9 million members in 212 countries today), the Mormons are ahead (7 million). Often the Mormons convey a more educated and cultured image—Brigham Young University, the Mormon Tabernacle Choir—than the Witnesses, who discourage higher education and whose most noted musician to date has been Michael Jackson.

Unlike the Mormons, Jehovah's Witnesses have added no new revelations to the Bible. But for all practical purposes their "Bible studies" take the place of the Bible.

History

Charles Taze Russell (1852-1916) was a successful Pennsylvania businessman, whose deep interest in religious matters moved him to leave the world of business and found a new religion. Dissatisfied with the churches of his day, Russell organized his own small Bible study group of which he became "pastor." In 1879 he first published *Zion's Watch Tower,* forerunner of today's semi-monthly magazine, *The Watchtower,* which boasts a printing of 13,950,000 each issue.

Russell's denial of the divinity of Jesus has remained a mainstay of Watchtower theology, as has his assertion that organized religion (except his own) is satanic. Russell's penchant for setting endtime dates has been another hallmark of the Watchtower over the years. In 1891, for instance, he predicted that 1914 would mark "the full establishment of the kingdom of God in the earth." The society explained this as an invisible return of Christ, even though the Bible says that "every eye will see him" (Revelation 1:7) when he returns.

Upon his death in 1916, Russell was followed by Judge Joseph Franklin Rutherford. An example of this man's boldness was his challenging the pope to a debate. He was ignored.

Like Russell, Rutherford wrote voluminously, publishing more than 100 books and pamphlets. In 1931 he gave the organization the name Jehovah's Witnesses, based on the American Standard Version translation of Isaiah 43:12: "Ye are my witnesses, saith Jehovah."

When Rutherford died in 1942, the Watchtower leadership passed to Nathan H. Knorr. Though lacking the flair of his predecessors, Knorr saw the organization grow from 115,000 members to over two million. During his presidency the society produced its own English translation of the Bible, the *New World Translation of the Holy Scriptures.* Witnesses consider this translation free from the "snare of religious traditionalism." Outsiders point to its wrong translations of key passages, especially those relating to the divinity of Jesus. The most noted of these is the New World translation of John 1:1 ". . . the Word was a god," instead of ". . . the Word was God."

In 1977 Frederick W. Franz became the society's fourth president. This now-elderly leader has seen the organization continue to grow.

Yet all is not well in the Watchtower. Recent years saw the much-publicized dismissal of the president's nephew, Raymond Franz, a member of the society's elite governing body. And a false prophecy concerning the end in 1975 led to the defection of hundreds of thousands of members.

Presently the Watchtower society is experiencing a tremendously high turnover rate. For every three members coming in, two are leaving or being "disfellowshiped." Meanwhile time is running out for what's left of the generation that witnessed 1914. According to the society, they would live to the end of this "system of things."

The Watchtower and *Awake!* magazines are published semimonthly. *The Watchtower* appears in 110 languages and boasts an average printing of over 15 million; *Awake!*, in 58 languages, averages 12 million.

Teachings

The Watchtower has had a knack for changing doctrines as it sees fit. One example of this involves Russell's prophecy about 1914. Prior to that date his *Studies in the Scriptures* read: ". . . the deliverance of the saints must take place sometime before 1914. . . ." The 1923 edition of the same volume says: ". . . the deliverance of the saints must take place *very soon after* 1914 . . ." (italics ours).

Nevertheless, certain of the Watchtower's unscriptural teachings have remained throughout the years. Jehovah's Witnesses deny the Trinity and the divinity of Jesus. They teach that he was Michael, the first Creation of Jehovah. They also deny the immortality of the soul and the reality of hell. Instead, they believe in the total annihilation of the ungodly. They contend that only 144,000 (the "little flock") will go to heaven; other believers (the "other sheep") will live in a paradise on earth. The Watchtower Society forbids military service and celebration of birthdays, Christmas, and other holidays. Witnesses are also known for their refusal to accept blood transfusions, based on their misunderstanding of Leviticus 17:10.

Just how do they come up with such unbiblical teachings? Witness theology tends to take Scripture passages out of context and then string them together to fit the society's ideas. One Bible scholar has likened it to stringing together the following passages: "(Judas) went away and hanged himself" (Matthew 27:5). "Go and do likewise" (Luke 10:37). "What you are about to do, do quickly" (John 13:27).

How do people get caught up in Watchtower doctrines? A revealing answer is given in the book *Thirty Years a Watchtower Slave,* written by an ex-Jehovah's Witness: "The Watchtower leadership sensed that within Christendom were millions of professing Christians who were not well grounded 'in the truths once delivered to the saints,' and would be rather easily pried loose from the churches and led into a new and revitalized Watchtower Organization. The Society calculated, and that rightly, that this would yield vast masses of men and women, if the whole matter were wisely attacked."

Witnessing to the Witnesses

Numerous ex-Jehovah's Witnesses, like Marilyn Zweifel of Milwaukee, speak of the difficulty of leaving the organization. She and her husband "disassociated" themselves after more than twenty years in the society. Now they are "shunned" as "apostates," and their own family members won't even talk to them. Mrs. Zweifel says that members are led to believe that "if you leave, you leave God." The organization is considered God's channel to earth.

Yet to remain in the religion is "scary." It means working feverishly to try to please Jehovah and his first Creation, Jesus, the awesome King who invisibly came to earth in 1914.

We can witness to these people. Don't slam the door on them. Don't try to argue; and don't let them jump around from one verse to another. Simply present Jesus Christ.

Jesus is God. Be well grounded in the many passages that point to his divinity, and be aware of how Witnesses may try to twist them. *Jesus is the Savior.* He has lived on earth for us, died, and risen again to bring us forgiveness, peace, and salvation. *Jesus is our Mediator.* Jesus, not any organization, is our access to God (1 Timothy 2:5,6). He has earned heaven for all people, not just for 144,000.

These are certainties that Christians have and Jehovah's Witnesses do not have. In love, then, let us be true witnesses of Jehovah, "while we wait for the blessed hope—the glorious appearing of our great God and Savior, Jesus Christ" (Titus 2:13).

> **Fingertip facts:**
>
> ***Founding:*** 1879 Pittsburgh, Pennsylvania, by Charles Taze Russell.
>
> ***Authority:*** The Bible study aids of the Watchtower Organization, including the *New World Translation.*
>
> ***Key teachings:*** Annihilation of the wicked; emphasis on end times.
>
> ***View of Bible:*** God's Word, but subject to Watchtower interpretation.
>
> ***View of Jesus:*** Michael, a created creature; the firstborn of God.
>
> ***View of Trinity:*** Father is Jehovah God; Jesus is a created being; Holy Spirit an impersonal force.
>
> ***Salvation:*** Christ's death provides the opportunity to work out our own salvation.

Further reading:

Kern, Herbert. *How to Respond to . . . the Jehovah's Witnesses* (part of the Concordia "Response Series"). St. Louis: Concordia, 1977.

Schnell, William J. *Thirty Years a Watchtower Slave.* Grand Rapids: Baker, 1971.

For study and discussion:

1. Discuss the basic differences between the Bible and the teachings of the Jehovah's Witnesses.

2. The *New World Translation of the Holy Scriptures* translates John 1:1: "In [the] beginning the Word was, and the Word was with God, and the Word was a god." Other translations

read, "The Word was God." The Word of course refers to Jesus Christ. What bias against Christ's divinity does the *New World Translation* show? Later in John 1 (verses 6,12,13,18) the same translation renders the same Greek term (*theos*, without the article) as "God"! How does the *New World Translation* rendering of John 1:1 square with Exodus 20:3? What are we to make of Christ if he is merely "a god"?

3. The Jehovah's Witnesses teach a strict morality (for example, no drinking). How might this impress prospective members?

4. How might the dedication and missionary zeal of Jehovah's Witnesses impress people?

5. Although the Jehovah's Witnesses are very active and growing, what does the high turnover rate say about the organization?

6. In *Thirty Years a Watchtower Slave*, former member William Schnell writes, "When you see the Jehovah's Witnesses, Christian, remember a few very important *don'ts*. Do not argue religion with the Witness, for his doctrines are built upon a misuse of the Bible. . . . Another *don't* is not to engage in a conversation about present events . . . . Don't buy literature or accept anything free from him. . . . Be courteous to the JW—let him continue his presentation without interruption on your part. But also, as the Witness from time to time asks you leading questions, *do not* answer them. . . . Finally, he is through . . . . Tell him what the Lord Jesus means to you: give him your testimony. Make it short and sweet, but say it with enthusiasm. Then ask the JW to give you his testimony. This will nonplus him—he cannot speak of the grace of God in Jesus Christ." Discuss the value of a positive witness for Christ.

7. In our lives and in our witnessing, note the value of our personal example. See 1 Peter 3:15,16.

4. Christian Science

On December 3, 1910, Mary Ann Morse Baker Glover Patterson Eddy died. The death of an eighty-nine-year-old woman ought be neither surprising nor unexpected. Mary Baker Eddy's death, however, was different.

This woman had denied the very reality of death and had founded a religion based upon that same denial. Today, more than eighty years after Mrs. Eddy's death, Christian Science lives on.

Mary Baker Eddy

The founder of Christian Science was born in Bow, New Hampshire, in 1821. Her parents belonged to a Congregationalist church that held strict Calvinist doctrines of predestination and hell. Much of her later teaching seemed to develop as a reaction to the idea of people being predestined to the fires of hell. In addition, her sickly childhood led to a preoccupation with physical health. Her life was further troubled with marital difficulties and mental suffering, leading to a quest for peace of mind.

In 1843 she married George Washington Glover. Although her husband died the next year, this marriage produced her only child, whom she sent to live with relatives. A second marriage, to a dentist named Daniel Patterson, ended in divorce. Her third marriage, in 1877, lasted and from it she received her final name, Eddy.

Mary Baker Eddy

Through her physical, mental, and emotional struggles and through contact with a mental healer named Phineas P. Quimby, Mrs. Eddy gradually developed her religion. The year 1866 was a turning point in her life. On February 1 of that year, she slipped on an icy sidewalk and was painfully injured. She later claimed that her doctor pronounced her fatally injured (a claim that he denied under oath) and that she recovered miraculously upon reading Matthew 9:2-8, the account of Jesus healing a paralyzed man.

According to Mrs. Eddy, this incident led to her "discovery" of what became known as Christian Science. Much evidence has been produced indicating that her book *Science and Health* was at least in part plagiarized from Quimby's work. First published in 1875, *Science and Health* is the foundational authority of her teaching; the title later included *With Key to the Scriptures*. In 1881 she established the "Massachusetts Metaphysical College," which became her "Church of Christ, Scientist," that is, Christian Science.

By the time she died, Mrs. Eddy was rich and famous. The skeptical Mark Twain—himself no friend of Christian Science—denounced her as a charlatan and yet called her "easily the most interesting person on the planet. . . ." Through sale of her book and her lessons she amassed a personal fortune of over $3 million.

But her wealth and renown did not bring her peace of mind. She was continually tormented by what she called Malicious Animal Magnetism. This evil disposition from others supposedly could bring sickness and death.

Science and Health

Just what legacy did this extraordinary woman leave to the world? We'll let her "inspired" book *Science and Health with Key to the Scriptures* speak for itself on a number of vital topics.

- The material world: "Matter has no life, hence it has no real existence" (p. 584).
- Sickness: "Man is never sick, for Mind is not sick and matter cannot be" (p. 393).
- Death: "An illusion, the lie of life in matter; the unreal and untrue; the opposite of Life" (p. 584).
- The Trinity: "The theory of three persons in one God . . . suggests polytheism, rather than the one ever-present I AM" (p. 256).
- Christ: "Christ, as the true spiritual idea, is the ideal of God now and forever" (p. 361). Elsewhere, in her *Miscellaneous Writings,* Mrs. Eddy states, "Jesus is not Christ."
- Jesus' death and resurrection: "Jesus' students, not sufficiently advanced fully to understand their Master's triumph, did not perform many wonderful works until they saw him after his crucifixion and learned that he had not died" (pp. 45-46).
- The Holy Spirit: "This Comforter I understand to be Divine Science" (p. 55).
- Sin: "But the belief in sin is punished so long as the belief lasts" (p. 497).
- The Bible's trustworthiness: Discussing Genesis 2:7: "Is it (man being formed from the dust) the truth or is it a lie concerning man and God? It must be a lie" (p. 524).

In his book *The Chaos of Cults,* Jan Van Baalen has described Christian Science as a religion "that, in veiled language and much double talk, teaches that Jesus was laid down, as a result of an apparent death, into a fictitious tomb, in an unreal body, to make an unnecessary atonement for sins that had never been a reality and had been committed in an imaginary body, and that he saves from non-existing evil those headed toward an imaginary hell, the false fancy of erroneous Mortal Mind."

To an age which tends to overlook the spiritual side of life and rely almost exclusively on physical solutions to its problems, Christian Science has something positive to offer. But, as Van Baalen puts it, that something is merely "the grain of truth in the bushel of error." With its denial of the material world and of basic biblical truths, Christian Science qualifies neither as science nor as Christian.

Christian Science today

The Christian Science church does not give out membership statistics. Nevertheless, on the basis of the number of congregations (also called branches) and practitioners (healers) it is possible to come up with some figures.

Apparently the cult reached its zenith in the 1930s and 40s. In 1941 there were an all time high 11,200 practitioners; by 1972 that had dropped to 5,848. According to a November 6, 1989 *U.S. News & World Report* article the church's present membership is estimated at less than 170,000, compared with about 270,000 prior to World War II. The church is centered in the U.S. but has branches in 37 countries.

One reason for the decline of Christian Science has been the much-publicized cases of children dying because their parents withheld medical treatment. In the summer of 1990 a case in Boston involved the two-year-old son of two devout Christian Scientists. The boy died of a bowel obstruction. He died in his father's lap and in the presence of a practitioner, whom the parents had called in for their child's spiritual healing.

Such cases have brought to the fore the question of religious rights. They have also cast grave doubts on the future of a religion that helps bring about such tragedies.

The Christian and Christian Science

In the face of its decline, the Christian Science church continues its work. It publishes the weekly *Christian Science Sentinel* magazine and the widely-acclaimed *Monitor* newspaper. Christian Science services are the same as in Mary Baker Eddy's day with readings from the Bible and *Science and Health*. And the omnipresent Christian Science reading rooms are still open with their fare of reading. Christian Scientists continue to rely on such means, rather than mass evangelism, for converts and income.

Even as Christian Science, "the matriarch of the Mind Science family," struggles, other "Science religions" carry on. Among them are L. Ron Hubbard's Church of Scientology and the Unity School of Christianity, which doesn't deny the reality of sin, sickness, and death but teaches that people have divine intelligence and can control their thoughts, feelings, and passions. This type of false Christianity, focusing on the mind rather than on the physical, goes back to the ancient heresy of gnosticism (Greek for "knowledge"). Truly, there is nothing new under the sun.

Perhaps Christian Science forces us to take a look at our own faith. Do we rely too much on the physical, the material? For one thing, let's not neglect prayer. We can pray for those caught in this sad religion.

If possible, witness. The solution to sin and death lies not in denying their existence. Rather, Jesus is the answer. In a real body he shed his blood and died for us. Then he physically rose to destroy the power of death itself. This knowledge helps us bear life's very real pains and gives us the certain hope of life in heaven.

Fingertip facts:

Founding: Around 1880 in New England by Mary Baker Eddy.
Authority: Science and Health with Key to the Scriptures.
Key teachings: Evil, the material world, sickness, and death have no real existence.
View of the Bible: Honored but put beneath *Science and Health*.
View of Jesus: Jesus Christ is not God.
View of the Trinity: Considered polytheistic.
Salvation: Since evil is unreal, salvation lies in having the right attitude.

Further reading:

Harm, Frederick. *How to Respond to . . . The Science Religions.* (part of the Concordia "Response Series"). St. Louis: Concordia, 1981.

Van Baalen, Jan. *The Chaos of Cults.* Grand Rapids: Wm. B. Eerdmans, 1962.

For study and discussion:
1. Review the basic differences between Christian Science and the Bible.

2. In what ways is Christian Science not scientific? In what ways is it not Christian?

3. Why might the Christian Science church be declining in influence in recent years? How might recent court cases affect the Christian Science church?

4. Rather than denying the existence of sin, what solution does the Bible offer? See Genesis 3:15.

5. Rather than denying the reality of suffering, how does the Bible deal with it? What purposes does suffering serve in the lives of Christians? See Zechariah 13:9; Hebrews 11—12.

6. The "science" religions stress healing and mind over matter. In their emphasis on the immaterial over the material world, they are greatly influenced by Eastern thought. Why might Westerners be receptive to religions that play down the physical and material side of life?

7. How does God want his people to show concern for both the physical and spiritual side of life? See Matthew 25:31-46; 28:19,20; James 2:14-17.

5.
The Unification Church

There are thousands of religious groups in the United States. Some of them are established worldwide religions, such as Hinduism, Islam, and Judaism. Each of these has its various divisions, as does Christianity with its denominations: Roman Catholic, Presbyterian, Lutheran, etc. In addition, newer breakaway groups, often referred to as sects, are constantly forming and dying off.

And then there are the cults, the new religions that don't fit in the other categories.

The term cult often has negative overtones. It brings to mind pictures of young people turning their backs on parents, isolating themselves in communes, and adopting strange anti-Christian beliefs. We also tend to think of mysterious leaders, spellbinding their devotees—some call it brainwashing. Perhaps images of Jim Jones and the tragic mass suicides of Jonestown in November 1978 flash before us.

Although the Jehovah's Witnesses and Mormons are cults, they've been around long enough for people to think of them as established religions. For many, the group that epitomizes the word cult is the Unification Church, whose followers are commonly called Moonies. Church leaders consider that term derogatory. They point to their official name, the Holy Spirit Association for the Unification of World Christianity. Whatever labels people might use, what's important is faithfulness to the word of God. Jesus said, "If you hold to my teaching, you are really my disciples" (John 8:31). An examination of the Unification Church shows it is not guided by the Holy Spirit, who works through the word of God. Nor is it a unifying factor or even Christian.

Characteristics

The Cult Awareness Network (CAN) is a non-religious organization dedicated to educating the public about what it calls "destructive cults." It defines a destructive cult as "a group with a hidden agenda of power through deceptive recruitment and complete control of the minds and lives of its members." CAN states that there are "well over 1000" such groups nationwide, with membership in the millions.

Although not all cults have exactly the same characteristics, there are many common threads running through them. A few are:

Deceit. A cult uses vagueness and secrecy about its goals and beliefs. Members rationalize this on the principle that the end justifies the means. The Unification Church (known on college campuses as CARP, the Collegiate Association for the Research of Principles) uses this "heavenly deception."

Love bombing. New recruits are touched, hugged, and flattered, so that they feel loved and important.

Renunciation. Former relationships with families and friends are renounced, and former values often referred to as "satanic."

Preoccupation with fund raising and recruiting. The Unification Church is known for its members selling flowers, candles, or candy on street corners and parking lots. In the book *Lord of the Second Advent* former Unification member Steve Kemperman recounts how he raised over $100,000 in three years in the mid 1970s.

Sleep deprivation. Long hours of recruiting and fundraising, as many as 20 hours per day, stifle critical thinking.

Charismatic, dogmatic leader. According to CAN, the "leader demands total devotion, and may claim supernatural power and unique, simple solutions to world problems."

Sun Myung Moon

In the case of the Unification Church, the absolute ruler is Sun Myung Moon. Born in Korea in 1920, Moon claims that when he was 16, Jesus appeared to him in a vision and informed him that the world would be transformed through Moon.

In 1945 Moon supposedly received another vision, which led to the founding of the Unification Church in 1954 in Seoul, Korea. An ardent anti-communist, Moon was twice imprisoned by the communists in that nine-year span.

During the 1970s Moon came to the United States where he carried out missionary activities and increased his already large business holdings. The year 1982 saw the famous mass wedding of 2,075 uniformly dressed couples, all followers of Moon, in Madison Square Garden. In 1984 he began serving an 18 month prison term for tax fraud. Nevertheless, Moon's financial empire has grown from $15 million in 1980 to $2 billion in 1990, and includes everything from weapon parts plants in South Korea to fishing co-ops in Louisiana to the *Washington Times* newspaper.

As of 1987 church membership estimates ranged from 5,000 to 15,000 in the United States and hundreds of thousands in Asia, especially Korea.

Although Moon's church claims to be Christian, his theology is anti-Christian to the core. According to the Unification "Bible," *Divine Principles,* Jesus failed in his mission on earth: "We must realize that through the crucifixion on the cross God and Jesus lost everything. . . . There was no redemption; there was no salvation; and there was no beginning of Christianity. So there on the cross, salvation was not given." The Unification Church also denies the bodily resurrection of Jesus.

The church considers Moon the Messiah. He has come to accomplish what Jesus failed to do. Through marriage, Moon will bring about a pure human race.

At heart, Unification theology—like that of all unbiblical religions—teaches work righteousness. People must earn their own salvation. Kemperman notes, "According to this Unification principle, salvation equals spiritual perfection (total oneness with God) which can only be achieved by man's constant 100 percent effort in both faith and action. Christianity on the other hand teaches that God's salvation is a gift."

Kemperman, who had been in the church for three and a half

years, also alludes to the vast difference between Moon and Jesus: "I had wanted to give him (Moon) a small, gift-wrapped box of chocolates.... When he'd finished his delivery and started heading out of the room, I pressed the gift against his right hand and said, 'Here, Father, for you.'

"Without flinching, or even looking aside, the glum-faced Father ignored my gift and bulldozed right past me into the dining room across the hall. So Sun Myung Moon remained for me an untouchable and distant man, a Messiah whom only the highest Church officials dared approach."

How different from Jesus who invites one and all, "Come to me, all you who are weary and burdened, and I will give you rest" (Matthew 11:28).

The Unification Church explains its emblem: "The circle in the center represents God, the twelve rays emanating from the center represent the twelve gates to the new Jerusalem ..., and the arrows encircling the symbol represent the universal give and take among God, man, and creation that is the basis for harmony and union."

One Unification training manual refers to Moon as "visible God." But the fact is that Sun Myung Moon is a false Messiah or Christ, of whom the true Christ warned, "At that time if anyone says to you, 'Look, here is the Christ!' or, 'There he is!' do not believe it. For false Christs and false prophets will appear..." (Matthew 24:23,24). We write this even though the Unification Church is known to sue those who speak against it.

Getting in and out

CAN literature indicates most people who join the cults are 16-35 years old, with the most vulnerable ages being 18-25. They generally come from middle to upper socioeconomic families, and are of average or higher than average intelligence. They are intellectually curious and idealistic, having philosophical questions about life. Many are also in a state of transition, off to school, away from home, in a new job, etc.

Another former member, Chris Elkins, points out that 70 percent of the Unification Church members are former members in mainline, established churches (from *What Do You Say to a Moonie?* Wheaton, IL: Tyndale House, 1981).

Elkins contends that these churches often lack a deep commitment to Scripture: ". . . in recent years some Christian churches have watered down their faith and simplified their theology. In an effort to make Christianity easier to accept, they have reduced it to mush." Some also lack an atmosphere of love and acceptance: "Many Moonies left the Christian church because they needed to be loved." Whether such comments are always warranted, this is how many people perceive the situation.

On the other hand, many do eventually leave the Unification Church; the turnover rate is very high. So if you know someone in this or another cult, don't stop praying, loving, and testifying.

Some are forcibly removed by the controversial "deprogrammers," whom Unification officials refer to as "thugs." Such tactics may border on the illegal and often don't bring a true change of heart.

A far better defense against the cults is that Christians and Christian churches be the loving, Christ-centered people God intends them to be. In these troubled times of false Christs, may we who know God's love in Jesus stand firm in his word, grow in that truth, and gladly share it with others.

Fingertip facts:

Founding: 1954 in Seoul, Korea, by Sun Myung Moon.
Authority: The writings of Sun Myung Moon.
Key teachings: Moon is the Messiah; purification of the human race.
View of the Bible: Reinterpreted through the Unification "Bible," *Divine Principles.*
View of Jesus: A man; a failed Messiah.
View of the Trinity: Unification theology is antitrinitarian; distinction between God and man blurred; man is "incarnate God."
Salvation: Earned through our own efforts.

Further reading:

Bjornstad, James. *Sun Myung Moon and the Unification Church.* Minneapolis: Bethany House, 1985.

Kemperman, Steve. *Lord of the Second Advent.* Ventura, CA: Regal Books, 1982.

Larson, Bob. *Larson's Book of Cults.* Wheaton, IL: Tyndale House, 1982.

For study and discussion:

1. Discuss the features that are typical of most new cults. Note especially the practice of "love bombing." How are Christian churches to show love? What is to be the motivation? See John 15:9-17; 1 John 4:7-21.

2. What other small cults have you read of or had some contact with?

3. Is it likely that the Unification church will continue to thrive and grow after the death of its founder? Do you think it will become another Mormon church or, like many other small groups, pass from the scene? What factors might make a difference?

4. Discuss the pros and cons of "deprogramming."

5. The box at the beginning of Lesson 1 recounts an Eckankar meeting which the author attended. Like the Unification church, Eckankar is a new cult. Eckankar was founded in 1965 by the late John Paul Twitchell and teaches the "ancient science of soul travel." What type of college student might be drawn into such small on-campus meetings?

6. What can churches do to reach out to people in cults such as the Unification Church? What can they do to keep young people close to their Christian faith, especially on college campuses?

7. What signs of the end times are clearly fulfilled in the claims of Sun Myung Moon and others like him? See Matthew 24:23-25.

6. The Muslims

Throughout history the Middle East has always managed to draw a great deal of attention. Along with modern oil wealth, that corner of our planet boasts the cradle of civilization, the backdrop for Bible history . . . and the birthplace of the world's second largest religion, Islam.

With some one billion followers, Islam is second in numbers only to the combined branches of Christianity, which total about a billion and a half. And with the fall of atheistic communism, Islam represents the greatest single challenge to the Christian faith as we approach the year 2000.

> Many names coming from Arabic have various English spellings. Some examples are: Madinah (Medina), Makkah (Mecca), Muhammad (Mohammed), Muslim (Moslem), Quran (Koran), Sura (Surah). This article follows the usage of the Islamic Affairs Department of Saudi Arabia.

Islamic resurgence

Although we tend to think of Islam in connection with the Middle East, less than 20 percent of today's Muslims live in the Arab world. The largest Islamic community is in Indonesia, and much of Africa is Muslim.

What may be especially startling and unsettling to Westerners, however, is the Muslim invasion of the West. France and

Great Britain, for example, have over 2.5 million Muslims each. Many of them are Turks, Indians, and Pakistanis who work in these European countries.

An article from the *Washington Times,* "Global Resurgence of Islam" (August 21, 1989), contrasts the new surge of Islam with the decline of much of the West:

"In West Germany . . . Turkish doctors, to support large Moslem families, work overtime aborting German women in a country where the average couple has but one child. At 60 million now, West Germany's population is expected to fall to 40 million in the new century. Berlin alone has 300,000 Moslems.

"In the U.S.S.R., Moslems number 50 million and are the fastest growing segment of the population, while the average Russian woman has five abortions."

There are between six and seven million Muslims in the U.S., including many African Americans. The Los Angeles area alone has some 400,000. That's about the size of the entire Wisconsin Evangelical Lutheran Synod.

Muhammad and the Quran

This aggressive, dynamic, and growing faith traces its roots to the prophet Muhammad (A.D. 570-632). Born in Makkah in southern Saudi Arabia, Muhammad tended sheep and camels as a youth, and later became a caravan merchant.

Having a strong religious bent, Muhammad would go out to a desert cave to fast and meditate for days at a time. On one such occasion, he claimed, the angel Gabriel appeared to him and related a message he was to share with the world.

This revelation was followed by numerous others for a period of twenty years. These "revelations," originally recited by Muhammad and later written down by his followers, make up the chapters, called "Suras," of the Muslims' holy book, the Quran.

The Quran is divided into 114 Suras and contains about 6,200 verses; it is about 85 percent the length of the New Testament. The Suras are not arranged chronologically. The opening prayer is first and then the longest chapters. Generally the shorter chapters (which are toward the end) are considered belonging to Muhammad's earlier years. Beginning at the end, then, and reading back toward the front would give the best idea of the development of Muhammad's teaching.

Muslims consider this book God's word. Like the Bible, the Quran teaches there is only one God. (The Muslim word for God, Allah, is related to the Old Testament Hebrew term El.) But it denies the Trinity.

It's clear that Muhammad had some knowledge of Christianity, perhaps gathered during merchant encounters with Arabian Christians. Yet it appears to have been a distorted knowledge. For example, the Quran depicts the triune God in this way: "And when Allah saith: O Jesus, son of Mary! Didst thou say unto mankind: Take me and my mother for two gods beside Allah? he saith: Be glorified! It was not mine to utter that to which I had no right . . ." (Sura 5:116). Here Mary is seen as a person in the Trinity. Although some see this verse as a refutation of Christian heresies which at Muhammad's time misrepresented the Trinity, the fact is that the Quran nowhere sets forth the biblical doctrine.

Minarets, from which the call to prayer is made, are a part of mosques. Like this one in Cairo, Egypt, they dominate the skyline of many Middle Eastern cities and are increasingly seen around the world.

Muhammad spoke of himself as the last and greatest in a line of prophets that included Moses and Jesus. The Quran has much to say about heaven and hell. Yet it teaches a work-righteousness and asserts that on judgment day people will be judged on the basis of their deeds.

As a matter of fact, it denies the very source of forgiveness, the crucifixion of Jesus: "They slew him (Jesus) not, but it appeared so unto them; and lo! those who disagree concerning it are in doubt thereof; . . . they slew him not for certain" (Sura 4:157).

To Muhammad, then, Jesus "was only a messenger

of Allah" (Sura 4:171), and not the eternal Son of God and Savior of the world.

Tragically, Islam's prophet flew in the face of biblical revelation, to which he claimed to have added the final word. For the Bible asserts, "But even if we or an angel from heaven should preach a gospel other than the one we preached to you, let him be eternally condemned!" (Galatians 1:8).

The Five Pillars

Islamic life centers around "the Five Pillars." Islam means "submission" and a Muslim is one who submits to expressions of Allah's will.

1. The Creed (Arabic, *Shahada*). "There is no God but Allah, and Muhammad is his prophet." Each Muslim must say this at least once in his lifetime. In reality, devout Muslims say it many times each day.
2. Ritual prayer (*Salat*). Prayers are said five times each day: at sunrise, noon, mid-afternoon, sunset, night. These prayers contain verses from the Quran, are recited in Arabic, said facing Makkah, and may be offered almost anywhere. On Fridays Muslims are to worship in the mosque.
3. Almsgiving (*Zakat*). Muslims are required to give $1/40$ ($2^1/_2$ percent) of their possessions wherever most needed, such as to the poor, debtors, slaves.
4. Fasting (*Sawm*). During the month of Ramadan, Muslims abstain from food, drink, and sexual relations from sunrise until sunset. This is considered a method of self-purification. The Muslims use a lunar calendar, so Ramadan rotates through the various seasons.
5. Pilgrimage (*Hajj*). If possible, each Muslim is to make a pilgrimage to Makkah during his lifetime. This includes a visit to Muhammad's tomb in Madinah, 260 miles north of Makkah. Every year some 2 million Muslims from around the globe make the hajj.

Some regard the *jihad* as a sixth pillar. The basic meaning of this word is "struggle for the faith." It has often been seen as a fight against unbelievers.

Muslims and Christians

Throughout the centuries, the relation between Islam and Christianity has been a struggle. Within a hundred years after the prophet's death, Muslim armies had conquered Spain and penetrated into France, only to be stopped at the battle of Tours in 732. We think also of the Crusades to win the Holy Land back from the Muslims. In Martin Luther's day the Turkish Muslims menaced Europe from the east, moving the Reformer to write the hymn "Lord, Keep Us Steadfast in Thy Word" as a prayer against the threatening Islamic armies.

Today the struggle continues. It is not to be won with arms or money. Rather, the victory lies in the word of God and prayer.

If indeed the Quran is a further revelation from God, then it ought to fulfill the Bible. Instead, as we have seen, the Quran contradicts God's word.

Islam is a simple, appealing faith. It does not make the difficult demands that Christ does, such as, "Be perfect, therefore, as your heavenly Father is perfect" (Matthew 5:48). But, then, it doesn't offer a Savior either.

Interestingly, the Quran urges Muhammad himself, "Ask forgiveness of thy sin" (Sura 40:55). Yet nowhere does it mention sin in connection with Jesus! The Quran offers a fallible prophet who lies buried in Arabia. The Bible presents a sinless Savior who has conquered death.

It behooves Christians to know something about Islam. Perhaps we should even do some reading in the Quran, so that we might better understand the Muslims.

Above all, let us submit to, serve, and proclaim him who "was delivered over to death for our sins and was raised to life for our justification" (Romans 4:25).

Fingertip facts:

Founding: A.D. 622 in Arabia by Muhammad.
Authority: The Quran.
Key teachings: The five pillars.
View of the Bible: God's revelation, superseded by the Quran.
View of Jesus: A great prophet, but not God.
View of the Trinity: Considered a false teaching.
Salvation: Man earns his own salvation.

Further reading:

Abdul-Haqq, Abdiyah Akbar. *Sharing Your Faith with a Muslim.* Minneapolis: Bethany Fellowship, 1980.

McDowell, Josh and Don Stewart. *Handbook of Today's Religions.* San Bernardino, CA: Here's Life Publishers, 1983.

Shorrosh, Anis A. *Islam Revealed.* Nashville: Thomas Nelson Publishers, 1988.

For study and discussion:

1. Islam considers Jews and Christians "people of the book." The Quran supposedly builds on the Bible and offers a further revelation. Discuss this in light of Galatians 1:8,9.

2. Within a hundred years after Muhammad's death, conquering Muslim armies had swept across north Africa and through Spain in the west and as far as the Indus River (India) in the east. While the conquered people were not forced to become Muslim, they were taxed more heavily. They also had to be impressed by the almost unbelievable conquests of Islam. What pressures and appeals might Islam have today as it continues to spread?

3. Muslims assert that the Comforter or Counselor (Greek, *Paraclete*) promised by Jesus refers to Muhammad. Read John 14:15-17; 15:26; 16:7-15. To whom do these passages clearly refer?

4. In Muhammad's day the Bible had not yet been translated into Arabic. What knowledge he had of the Old and New Testaments he picked up from Jews and Christians he encountered. With what biblical character does he seem to confuse Mary, the mother of Jesus, in the following passages? "O Mary! . . . Oh sister of Aaron! . . . (Sura 19:27,28). "Mary, daughter of Imran . . ." (Sura 66:12). See Numbers 26:59.

5. Islam allows men to have four wives (Muhammad himself by special dispensation had a dozen). Several Quranic verses from Sura 4, entitled "Women," indicate Muslim attitudes toward women: "Allah chargeth you concerning (the provision for) your children: to the male the equivalent of the portion of two females" (Sura 4:11). "Men are in charge of women, because Allah hath made the one of them to excel the other, and because they spend of their property (for the support of women). So good women are the obedient, guarding in secret that which Allah hath guarded. As for those from whom ye fear rebellion, admonish them and banish them to beds apart, and scourge them. Then if they obey you, seek not a way against them. Lo! Allah is ever High Exalted, Great" (Sura 4:34). Compare such verses with Ephesians 5:22-33; 1 Peter 3:1-7.

6. It is of interest that strongly Islamic countries, such as Saudi Arabia, are closed to Christian mission work, while the West is wide open to Muslim efforts. Yet Muslims are coming to Christ. (It's estimated that over half of all Christian converts from Islam are Indonesian.) What does this tell us of the power of the gospel? How should it encourage us to support overseas missions, many of which encounter Islam? See Romans 1:16; 1 Corinthians 1:18-25; Colossians 4:2-4.

7. In what ways is Jesus Christ far greater than the prophets and apostles of the Bible and the prophet of Islam, Muhammad? Although Islam claims to honor Jesus, how does it really dishonor him? See John 5:22,23.

7.
Baha'i

We might expect that a religion as old and as large as Islam would have its share of divisions. And that is just the case.

While the vast majority (about 85 percent) of Muslims are *Sunnis,* that is, orthodox, millions are found in numerous other groups. One early movement which continues to this day is that of the *Sufis.* This group is known for its asceticism, mysticism, and whirling dervishes. The *Ahmadiyya* Muslim movement dates from the last century and comes from India, but has made itself heard in the West. The *World Community of Islam* in the West, formerly known as the Black Muslims, began in 1930.

The Shiites and the Bab

Next to the Sunnis, the largest single group is the *Shiites* (about 12 percent). This is the religion of Iran, ancient Persia.

The Shiites trace their origin back to Muhammad's son-in-law, Ali (died 661), and since that time have differed with the Sunnis over the spiritual leadership of Islam. According to Shiite belief, Ali had twelve descendants who were the legitimate heads of Islam. These men were known as Imams (teachers) and also called "gates," that is, gates to the true faith. In A.D. 872 the twelfth and most revered Imam disappeared. Since then, Shiites have been waiting for him to return and lead them to world conquest.

In 1844 a young Persian named Mirza Ali Muhammad stepped forth and declared himself the Imam and the Bab, Persian for gate. This claim set the country on fire. In the persecutions that befell the Bab and his followers, he was executed in 1850 at the age of thirty.

Baha'u'llah and the Baha'is

The Bab's religion might have died with him, had it not been for one of his loyal followers, Mirza Husayn Ali. The Bab had claimed to be the last in a long line of prophets, beginning with Adam and including Jesus and Muhammad. The Bab was to be the founder of a new religion, Babism, which would conquer the world. But someday, declared the Bab, another great prophet would arise.

Mirza Husayn Ali Baha'u'llah

Less than twenty years after the Bab's death, Husayn Ali declared himself to be that prophet, "chosen by God, and the promised one of all the prophets." He took the name "Baha'u'llah," which means Glory of God.

Like the Bab, Baha'u'llah suffered persecution. He died in 1892 in Akko, Palestine, where he had been exiled. His son Abdul Baha came to America in the early part of this century to secure a Baha'i beachhead here.

Since the death of Abdul Baha's grandson, Shoghi Effendi, in 1957, the Baha'is are no longer governed by a descendant of Baha'u'llah, but by an elected body of representatives from around the globe.

Today there are some 360,000 Baha'is in North America, and 5.3 million in 200 countries worldwide. Baha'i life centers around local councils, called "spiritual assemblies." The U.S. has 1700 such assemblies and there are 25,000 around the world. The Baha'is hold weekly "firesides," informal meetings in private homes. Baha'i literature has been published in 800 languages.

Baha'i beliefs and teachings

In some respects the Baha'i Faith today is far removed from its Muslim origins. Unlike Islam, which is an exclusive faith,

Baha'ism is ecumenical and attempts to unite all religions.

According to a Baha'i brochure, the following are "among the most fundamental of Baha'i beliefs":

- There is only one God.
- All religions share a common foundation. "All the prophets of God proclaim the same faith."
- Mankind is one. People of all races, nations, economic groups, and religious backgrounds are equal in the sight of God.

The brochure, "Welcome to the Baha'i House of Worship," goes on to state that Baha'u'llah brought these teachings "to guide modern man":

The beautiful Baha'i House of Worship in Wilmette, Illinois. The nine-sided building reflects the symbolic number nine which, among other things, represents what Baha'is consider the world's nine living religions.

- the independent investigation of truth
- the essential harmony of science and religion
- the equality of men and women
- universal compulsory education
- a spiritual solution to the economic problem
- a universal auxiliary language
- a universal peace upheld by a world government.

Such beliefs and teachings make for appealing platitudes. But do they stand up?

To get to the "common foundation" of all religions, the Baha'i Faith must deny or ignore fundamental differences among the world's religions. Take, for example, the contrasting views of God among some of the religious leaders whom Baha'is consider manifestations of the divine: Zoroaster proclaimed two supreme beings; Buddha held that God is not relevant; and Jesus and the Bible teach a personal, triune God.

The Baha'i emphasis on "independent investigation of truth" is also open to question. Nearly a century after Baha'u'llah's death, Baha'is have yet to translate his "Most Holy Book," *Al-Kitab Al-Aqdas,* and thus make it accessible for those who wish to investigate. Baha'is do follow certain of its injunctions, such as having a year consisting of 19 months of 19 days each, beginning on March 21. Other teachings might prove an embarrassment, especially in the West. The Aqdas allows men to have two wives; and elsewhere it legislates, "Whoever burns a house intentionally, burn him" (translation from the original Arabic by Earl Elder and William McElwee Miller).

Baha'u'llah and Christ

Baha'ism minimizes the miracles of Jesus Christ, and denies his work of atonement on the cross, his physical resurrection, his glorious return, the resurrection of the body, the existence of the devil and of hell. In effect, it denies almost every biblical teaching.

Baha'is today may visit the tomb of Baha'u'llah in Akko and those of the Bab and Abdul Baha on Mount Carmel in nearby Haifa. Were these pilgrims to travel seventy miles south and visit Jerusalem, they might learn more of the One who was buried there and rose on the third day.

Baha'u'llah wanted to bring world peace, yet the world remains in turmoil. Jesus came to bring peace between the sinner and God, and millions continue to find that peace which the world cannot give. Baha'u'llah tried to unite the world under his laws and religion, but has only succeeded in adding to this weary planet more spiritual legislation and another religion. Christ came not to bring more laws and "condemn the world, but to save the world" (John 3:17). To life's weary pilgrims he says, "Come to me . . . and you will find rest for your souls" (Matthew 11:28,29).

Let us invite our Baha'i friends and others to learn more of Jesus. In his perfect life, sacrificial death, and resplendent resurrection he is the true glory of God. Indeed, he is the gate to God, to heaven, and to life without end!

> **Fingertip facts:**
> ***Founding:*** Mid nineteenth century Persia by Mirza Husayn Ali (Baha'u'llah).
> ***Authority:*** The writings of Baha'u'llah, Abdul Baha, Shoghi Effendi.
> ***Key teachings:*** Oneness of God, religion, humankind.
> ***View of the Bible:*** Quoted for Baha'i purposes, but not authoritative for people today; not considered inerrant.
> ***View of Jesus:*** "The prophet of the Christians" for that era, but now we are to follow Baha'u'llah.
> ***View of the Trinity:*** Denied.
> ***Salvation:*** Through human effort.

Further reading:

Beckwith, Francis. *Baha'i.* Minneapolis: Bethany House, 1985.

Miller, William McElwee. *The Baha'i Faith.* Pasadena, CA: William Carey Library, 1974.

For study and discussion:

1. Note the major differences between the teachings of the Baha'i Faith and the Bible.

2. Baha'is emphasize "unity of all religions." Even in comparing non-Christian religions such as the Unification Church and Islam, what great disunity do we find? What does the Bible say about Jesus being but one of many ways to God? See John 14:6; Acts 4:12.

3. Many people judge the truth of a cause by the conviction of those holding it. The Bab died a martyr for the religion he founded. How did this affect the truth of his revelation? How might it affect people who are looking into Baha'ism?

4. Note the appeal of Baha'i beliefs and teachings for modern man. What do they fail to take into account in setting forth these lofty goals? See Romans 3:10-12,23.

5. Someone has noted, "There is a snag in the statement . . . of the Baha'is that all religions are basically one and the same, and are equally good, therefore join . . . the Baha'is on that basis. If they are all the same, why another?" In what ways is the Baha'i Faith simply another religion among many? In what ways is Christianity unique among all religions?

6. According to the 1923 edition of the Baha'i book *Baha'u'llah and the New Era* (by J. E. Esslemont. New York: Baha'i Publishing Committee), Abdul Baha referred to the year 1957 and predicted, "Universal Peace will be firmly established, a Universal language promoted. Misunderstandings will pass away. The Baha'i cause will be promulgated in all parts and the oneness of mankind established!" In the 1970 edition of this book the prophecy is deleted. What does this kind of change say about the sincerity of the Baha'i teaching of "independent investigation of truth"? What does Abdul Baha's prophecy say about his credentials as a prophet? See Deuteronomy 18:21,22.

7. Baha'is say that the prophecy of Isaiah 9:6,7 could not refer to Jesus because "the government" was not "on his shoulders." They also say that Jesus did not claim to be the "Prince of Peace" and that he was not known as the "Father." Rather, they contend, it refers to Baha'u'llah. How has Jesus indeed fulfilled the prophecy? Read Isaiah 9:6,7; Matthew 28:18; John 14:9,10,27; 16:33. Isaiah stated that the coming Savior would "reign on David's throne . . . forever." According to 2 Samuel 7:12,13, whose descendant would have such an everlasting kingdom? How did Jesus, and not Baha'u'llah, fulfill this? See Matthew 1:1.

8.
Hinduism

*Oh, East is East, and West is West,
and never the twain shall meet....*

Rudyard Kipling's famous lines are an apt description of the vast gulf separating the ways and thoughts of the Western world from those of the East. Nowhere is this more evident than in a comparison of the foremost religion of India, Hinduism, with biblical Christianity.

Hindu thought and life

Hinduism's roots go back to about 1500 B.C., close to the time of Moses. Ancient Hinduism, as found in the writings known as the *Rig Vega,* was polytheistic; that is, it held to a belief in many gods, as did many religions of that time.

Over the centuries the Hindu religion has evolved into a very complex system of thought and way of life. Several basic themes undergird today's Hinduism and have profound impact on Hindu life.

One of those central themes is *pantheism,* the belief that the entire universe is a part of "God." Even if we are not aware of it, we are a fragment of "God." In contrast, the Bible teaches that God, the Creator, is distinct from his creation. Moreover, the Hindu "God," often referred to as Brahman, is an impersonal force, quite unlike the personal God we worship and to whom we pray.

The Hindu ideal is to be absorbed into the ultimate reality of Brahman and to be free from this present material world, which is considered merely an illusion. This leads to a second fundamental belief of Hinduism—reincarnation.

Hindu teaching contends that "a man has a soul, and it passes from life to life, as a traveler from inn to inn." The doctrine of reincarnation, also known as *samsara* (wandering), rebirth, or transmigration, is at odds with the Bible's assertion, ". . . man is destined to die once, and after that to face judgment" (Hebrews 9: 27).

According to Hindu thought, an individual passes through thousands of reincarnations until he is finally released from this dreary bondage into union with Brahman. This union (called *moksha*) is likened to a drop of water being absorbed into the ocean.

Hindu temple in Madras, India

People's accumulation of *karma*—their good and bad deeds—determines where they will spend their next reincarnation. Closely tied to reincarnation and *karma,* the Hindu caste system has locked the people of India into a fatalistic resignation to the social class into which they are born. To see firsthand the squalor, filth, and disease everywhere present in India is to get some notion of where Hindu thought leads.

The three ways

Hinduism teaches three ways of attaining release from the almost endless chain of reincarnation. Each way lays on people the heavy burden that they must save themselves, whereas the Bible presents the good news that salvation is "the gift of God—not by works" (Ephesians 2:8,9).

The first is the way of knowledge (*jnana-marga*). This way includes meditation and reasoning. Relatively few, such as the Hindu monks, follow this intellectual way.

The second is the way of works (*karma-marga*). Good works are performed to achieve release into the eternal.

The most popular path is the way of devotion *(bhakti-marga)*. Most Hindus devote themselves to the worship of some manifestation of Brahman. Although in theory Hinduism is pantheistic, in practice among the masses of people it is polytheistic, having some 30 million different gods. I recall a conversation I once had with a Hindu in India; he was very happy to accept Jesus as another among many gods—but not as *the* way.

In following these ways, Hindu life revolves around several practices. One is *puja,* the offering of flowers and food to the gods. Another is meditation on a *mantra,* a sacred word or phrase spoken over and over. A third practice is *yoga,* the use of meditation and physical discipline to gain self-mastery.

Hinduism in the West

According to 1992 statistics, there are 705,000,000 Hindus worldwide, making Hinduism the third largest religion in the world after Christianity and Islam. All but about 5 million Hindus live in south Asia, especially India. Some 1,250,000 reside in North America.

Hinduism's impact in North America goes back about 100 years. In 1893 Swami Vivekananda of India made an impressive appearance at the Parliament of World Religions in Chicago.

The years following Vivekananda have seen an influx of other swamis, more commonly known as gurus. These men are regarded as spiritual masters, who have supposedly reached the end of their many thousands of reincarnations. They share their vast store of accumulated spiritual insights with their devotees.

Recent decades have seen a number of gurus gain notoriety in the United States. To name but three: Maharishi Mahesh Yogi (founder of Transcendental Meditation), A. C. Bhaktivedanta Prabhupada (Hare Krishna), and Maharaj Ji (Divine Light Mission). These and other gurus have risen and then passed from prominence, either through death or loss of credibility.

Yet Hinduism's influence in the West continues to grow, far outweighing the actual numbers of Hindus. Key Hindu concepts have become household terms and, what is more, been absorbed into the belief systems of countless Westerners. For example, at the turn of the century only one or two percent of people in Europe and North America believed in reincarnation; by 1982 that figure was about 22 percent.

The so-called New Age Movement has done much to help further Hindu ideas (see Lesson 9). Shirley MacLaine and other New Age advocates have popularized notions such as, "You are God." On one occasion, when challenged as to her divinity, MacLaine responded, "If you don't see me as God, it's because you don't see yourself as God."

In this way the biblical concept of sin and salvation has been undermined. Humanity's basic problem is not seen as sin, but as the lack of knowledge. Once we realize we are God, we can get on the path to salvation.

Christians and Hinduism

As the West continues to lose its grip on once commonly-held Christian truths, believers need to stand firm. We need to know the Bible. We need to know the differences between falsehood and biblical truth, and then share that truth in love.

The difference between Hinduism and Christianity is not really Eastern versus Western world views. Nor is it simply a matter of cultural or philosophical differences. It is a question of who is God. The Hindu god, of which we are supposedly a part, is a vague impersonal force. But Jesus Christ has shown himself to be God incarnate, victor over sin, death, and the forces of hell. On the last day he will visibly return to judge his creation. As Kipling's poem continues:

> *Oh, East is East, and West is West,*
> *and never the twain shall meet,*
> *Till earth and sky stand presently*
> *at God's great judgment seat.*

> **Fingertip facts:**
> *Founding:* About 1500 B.C. in the Indus Valley, India.
> *Authority:* Hindu scriptures (*Veda*); other Hindu literature (*Smriti*).
> *Key teachings:* Pantheism; reincarnation.
> *View of Bible:* Another sacred scripture along with the Hindu scriptures.
> *View of Jesus:* He is god as all people are god; a guru.
> *View of Trinity:* There are many manifestations of God.
> *Salvation:* We must save ourselves.

Further reading:

Albrecht, Mark. *Reincarnation, A Christian Appraisal.* Downers Grove, IL: InterVarsity Press, 1982.

Johnson, David. *A Reasoned Look at Asian Religions.* Minneapolis: Bethany House, 1985.

For study and discussion:

1. In what key ways does Hinduism differ from Christianity? Why can there be no coming together of the two religions?

2. How is pantheism diametrically opposed to the biblical teaching of the nature of God and creation? See Genesis 1:1. What important difference is there between pantheism and the omnipresence of God? See Psalm 139:7-12. How does pantheism affect the doctrine of sin?

3. Sometimes Hindus point to Jesus' words in Luke 17:21, "the kingdom of God is within you," as teaching pantheism. What is Jesus talking about here? Consider the context, Luke 17:20,21, and passages such as Matthew 23:25,26; John 18:36.

4. What factors in Hinduism might lead people to a very pessimistic, fatalistic view of life?

5. Why does the Hindu life of meditation and consciousness seem to balance the Western (not necessarily Christian) emphasis on the active life?

6. At times a distinction is made between *transmigration* and *reincarnation*. The former is used for the ancient Indian-Hindu concept that people can pass from this life into lower life forms (plants, animals). The latter is used for the Westernized concept that people only pass into other human lives. Why would the more purely Hindu concept be unappealing in the West?

7. Some say that Jesus' words in Matthew 11:14 teach reincarnation: "[John the Baptist] is the Elijah who was to come." What is Jesus teaching here? Consider the context, Matthew 11:7-14, as well as other passages, Luke 1:17; John 1:21. Does Jesus teach reincarnation when he says, "I tell you the truth, no one can see the kingdom of God unless he is born again" (John 3:3)? Look at the context, John 3:1-12; also John 1:12,13; 1 Peter 1:23.

9. The New Age Movement

> *This is the dawning of the age of Aquarius,*
> *When the moon is in the seventh house*
> *And Jupiter aligns with Mars,*
> *Then peace will guide the planets*
> *And love will steer the stars.*

These words from the 1970s musical *Hair* told the public that the world was entering a new era. According to astrologers, for two thousand years our planet has been under Pisces, the sign of the fish (see lesson 10 on Astrology). What many have seen as an era of violence and disillusionment, beginning with the death of Christ, is supposedly giving way to a time of joy and aspiration. As the song goes on, it will be a time for "the mind's true liberation."

We are said to be on the verge of the Age of Aquarius, better known as the *New Age*.

New Age roots

The roots of the New Age and the forces that give impetus to the New Age Movement (NAM) are many. At first blush NAM might appear to be a confusing kaleidoscope of influences and ideas. Yet as we look at some of that multi-colored background, certain patterns emerge and we are able to arrive at an understanding of the movement.

The strongest single influence on NAM is Hinduism (see lesson 8), with its teachings of pantheism and reincarnation. Buddhism, an offshoot of Hinduism, has influenced NAM with its emphasis on intuitive knowledge over logic and reason. Another source is the ancient Christian heresy of gnosticism, stressing the possession of insider, esoteric knowledge.

NAM also mixes in Native American ideas of the medicine man (the shaman), as popularized in the writings of Carlos Castaneda (*Journey to Ixtlan,* etc.). Nineteenth century American spiritualists who claimed to communicate with the dead were New Age forerunners. So were the German hypnotist Franz Anton Mesmer (1734-1815), from whom we get the term "mesmerize," and the healer Phineas P. Quimby, a mentor of Mary Baker Eddy (see lesson 4).

Add to this a measure of the occult, with its delving into hidden, secret things through fortune-telling, magic, and mediums. Mix in a strong dosage of secular psychology with the stress on self: self-love, self-esteem, self-image, self-actualization, self-fulfillment. Stir in some ancient paganism, such as the worship of mother earth, *Gaia*—and you have the New Age.

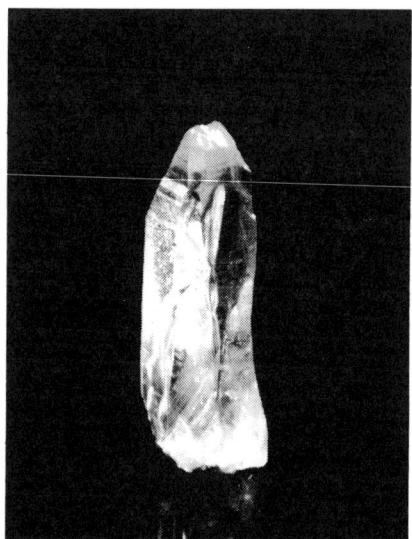

The crystal, symbol of the New Age. These quartz rocks have very predictable vibratory qualities, which make them useful in science. New Agers believe that crystals can also channel wholesome vibrations into the human mind, body, and emotions.

Although the New Age Movement has been stirring in the Western world for over a century, in recent years it has begun to boil over into society at large. In the fifties, it was still a movement of outsiders. The Beatniks—a la Jack Kerouac, Allen Ginsberg—turned their backs on society's stale materialism. They experimented with drugs, free sex, and Eastern religion. Then, in the sixties, came the Hippies, flower children with their communes, more drugs, meditation, and gurus from India.

The year 1971 has been referred to as the movement's "galvanization date," when it entered into the mainstream of American society. That year marked the first publication of the periodical *East-West Journal*. It also ushered in the first truly representative book, *Be Here Now*, by Baba Ram Dass, Jewish-born Richard Alpert. This former Harvard professor and coworker of Timothy Leary of LSD fame recounted his journey from professor, into the world of psychedelic drugs, and then into becoming a practitioner of yoga, a yogi.

Ram Dass's journey into Eastern mysticism is one that more and more are following.

New Age thinking

When we consider this varied, kaleidoscopic tapestry called the New Age, just what are the common patterns running through the entire movement? There are several basic threads.

One is the concept of *pantheism*. Everything is God. This of course means that people are also divine. "Kneel to your own self. Honor and worship your own being. God dwells in you as you." These words of Swami Muktananda sum up what the New Age is all about.

Surprisingly, New Age pantheism is very close to the secular, godless humanism that for many years dominated Western society. Both place human beings at the center of existence. Humanism does so because it asserts there is no God; the New Age Movement does so because *we* are God. In the end there's little difference between the two. Except this: God, the true God, has created us as spiritual beings. A philosophy of life that completely disregards the spiritual aspect cannot hold people. Along with the weakening of secular humanism, the collapse of atheistic communism is another example of this. On the other hand, a world view that not only deals with spiritual matters but tells us we are divine is very appealing.

Pantheism really has no values to offer. If everything is divine, then in one way or another everything is all right. No one can say that anything is wrong. Today's moral confusion is an indication of how deeply such thinking has permeated society. We are thrown back on our own ideas and feelings to determine values. Everyone creates his or her own reality, one's own universe. Hand in hand with pantheism goes *reincarnation*. According to secular humanism, individual human potential ends at death. Not so with the New Age where we last forever. We are divine and must pass from one temporal body into another. If we have problems, it's because at some level, perhaps unconsciously or in a previous life, we have willed it. Thus if a baby dies, it's because the child brought it about.

A third New Age emphasis is on *consciousness*. According to New Age thought, mankind's problem is not sin, but lack of knowledge. The problem is that we need to be conscious of our divinity. Shirley MacLaine, who has done as much as anyone to popularize New Age thought, puts it this way: "Just remember that you are God, and act accordingly." What New Agers don't satisfactorily answer is why, if we are God, do we have to be told about it? Why do people need to spend several hundred dollars for a weekend seminar with MacLaine to learn this?

At any rate, this need for consciousness leads to a fourth New Age tenet: *transformation*. Somehow we need to break through from old ways of thinking into the awareness of our divinity. We need to be transformed; our consciousness needs to be altered. When enough individuals are transformed, there will be global transformation.

New Age practices and promotion

There are many techniques available for this transformation. It doesn't matter so much which one you follow as long as you somehow make the shift into the new consciousness. And that's where the many New Age techniques and practices come into play.

Techniques for altering consciousness include chanting, primal therapy, dream therapy, body disciplines, diet, yoga, drugs, acupuncture, channeling (contacting the dead through mediums), hypnosis, crystals, holistic healing, etc. An army of therapists, psychics, channelers, and gurus stands ready (for a price) to help the novice make the journey into an altered state of consciousness.

Not everyone involved in the New Age makes use of all these means. Nor is everyone who uses them aware of their New Age connections. For example, many who practice yoga may be unaware that it is intimately tied with the New Age and Hindu thought. Numerous large companies involve their employees in training seminars which espouse New Age principles, such as creating one's own values or looking inward for success.

Many people are subtly introduced to the New Age when they become involved in Transcendental Meditation or various self-improvement seminars.

Moreover, a number of New Age causes are ones which Christians would to some degree endorse. Yet the New Age mindset from which they come is completely different and headed in another direction. The New Age concern for the environment and ecology, for instance, springs not from a Christian concern for being good stewards of God's creation. Rather, it comes from the notion that we are one with *Gaia,* mother earth. In this schema human beings are a part of nature as are whales; and while it may be important to fight for whales as an endangered species, human abortion may be perfectly acceptable as a means of keeping a balance in nature. The biblical idea of people subduing the earth and ruling over the animals (Genesis 1:28) is foreign to the New Age.

New Ager Marilyn Ferguson correctly notes that NAM "has infected medicine, education, social science, hard science, even government with it implications" (*The Aquarian Conspiracy.* Los Angeles: J. P. Tarcher, 1980). Meanwhile, George Lucas's Star Wars movies have spread the New Age concept of "the Force," a power we can tap into by reaching within ourselves. And already in 1987 America's major corporations were putting "about $4 billion in corporate spending" into New Age self-improvement programs for employees (*Newsweek,* 5/4/87).

Age-old lies

Some see a conspiracy behind the entire New Age Movement. The fact is that NAM is hardly an organized movement. Some who share New Age ideals don't even like the label, because it can carry negative, even eccentric connotations. Far from being simply another organization or new cult, NAM encompasses people from many religions, cults, and organizations. NAM represents not so much any one organization as a way of thinking. It is the ushering in of a new consciousness, the awareness of our divinity.

In another way, however, NAM is a conspiracy. The devil is behind it. The lure of godhead is Satan's age-old lie from the Garden of Eden: "You will be like God, knowing good and evil" (Genesis 3:5). As Shirley MacLaine puts it, "We already know everything. The knowingness of our divinity is the highest intelligence."

This ancient lie of Satan will not bring the enlightenment and liberation it offers. Only Jesus Christ can do that. He who has died and risen again offers the best and only real assurance for this or any other age: "Surely I am with you always, to the very end of the age" (Matthew 28:20).

Fingertip facts:

Founding: 1971 with the publication of the *East-West Journal* and Baba Ram Dass's *Be Here Now*.

Authority: The self.

Key teachings: Oneness of all things; need for altered consciousness.

View of Bible: Not really necessary; just one of many paths.

View of Jesus: Different from Christ; Jesus was a man; Christ is but the Christian name for the great world teacher, Lord Maitreya.

View of Trinity: The personal God of Scripture is replaced by an impersonal Force.

Salvation: Not from sin and hell, but from disharmony; not by grace, but by human effort.

Further reading:

Groothuis, Douglas R. *Unmasking the New Age.* Downers Grove, IL: InterVarsity Press, 1986.

Hunt, Dave and T. A. McMahon. *America: The Sorcerer's New Apprentice.* Eugene, OR: Harvest House Publishers, 1988. (Hunt is also featured in the video *Gods of the New Age*.)

Larson, Bob. *Straight Answers on the New Age.* Nashville: Thomas Nelson Publishers, 1989.

For study and discussion:

1. In what ways and in what areas has New Age thought influenced modern society?

2. Among other things, the New Age is a reaction to religious pluralism. Rather than trying to distinguish differences among the many religions that now exist side by side in our "global village," more and more people simply see them all as various expressions of God and basic spiritual truths. What problems does this have? See Exodus 20:3; Psalm 96:4,5; John 14:6,7.

3. The New Age Movement (NAM) has many similarities with humanism (the focus on self, faith in human potentiality, antagonism toward biblical truth, etc.). Why might we expect to see more of the openly *spiritual* side of NAM and less purely *secular* humanism in the future?

4. Why, in our scientific age, would so many people turn to fortunetelling, the occult, astrology, Eastern mysticism, nature worship, and other "new" age practices which are really nothing but a return to ancient paganism?

5. Although the New Age Movement teaches people to look inside themselves, at the same time many New Agers look to astrology for guidance. What does this tell us about man's inability to find direction and purpose in life entirely from within himself?

6. According to *Newsweek* magazine (2/3/92), more and more people are replacing aerobic workouts with yoga. In gyms

"where once was heard the throbbing beat of [aerobic music] ... New Age woodwinds now reign." For some, it is a "spiritual elevation" and one instructor "was pleased to find her students readily took to the traditional [Hindu] 'Om' chant before and after class." Discuss how yoga classes and other seemingly innocent activities can be spiritually harmful and lead to deeper involvement in the New Age.

7. Compare with NAM the manner in which Satan lured our first parents with the promise of special knowledge and godhead. See Genesis 3. What does God say about the NAM practice of placing the creature in place of the Creator? Where does it lead? See Romans 1:18-32. Wherein does true transformation lie? What is its source? See Romans 12:1,2; 2 Corinthians 5:14,15.

10.
Astrology

According to *Webster's New World Dictionary* astrology is "(1) originally, primitive astronomy (2) a pseudoscience claiming to foretell the future by studying the supposed influence of the relative positions of the moon, sun, and stars on human affairs."

A modern astrologer defines it this way: "Astrology . . . is shown to have been essentially, from the very dawn of human civilization, *the result of man's attempt to understand the apparent confusion and chaos of his life-experiences by referring them to the ordered patterns of cyclic activity which he discovers in the sky*" (Italics are the author's. Dane Rudhyar, *The Practice of Astrology*. The Netherlands: Servire/Wassenaar, 1968).

Astrology then and now

Astrology has been traced back to the ancient Chaldeans and Babylonians of about 3000 B.C. At first astrology was concerned with observing and recording data about the heavenly bodies. (Today this is the purpose of astronomy.) Gradually the stars and planets came to be regarded as supernatural beings, gods whose movements were equated with divine actions. The ancients worshiped the heavenly bodies and looked to them for guidance.

Modern astrology's connection with the ancient gods is not always apparent. But the heavenly bodies are still thought to influence and foretell events on earth in a godlike, supernatural manner. In the East, astrology is an integral part of daily life.

For example, in India more than 60 percent of the population regularly consults astrologers.

In the Western world, it has become big business. As many as 50 million Americans, mostly women, look at the alignment of stars for guidance. Some are casual seekers; others are in earnest. A "conservative" 1983 estimate asserted that 175,000 part-time and 10,000 full-time astrologers practice in the United States. These numbers may well be much higher today. Horoscopes (daily astrological forecasts based on a person's birth date) appear in more than 2000 U.S. newspapers.

Someone has remarked, "History has shown that astrology thrives best in times of religious decline and of social unrest." The troubled times in which we live account for many people, including many churchgoers, looking to the stars for answers to the future.

Signs of the zodiac

"What's your sign?" has become a common conversation starter. Some 80 percent of Americans are able to answer that query. For the few who are still among the uninformed, the "sign" is one of the 12 divisions of the zodiac, each represented by a symbol.

The zodiac is an imaginary belt in the heavens along which the sun appears to travel. If your birthday is between July 23 and August 22 your "sign" is Leo, the lion. This means you are likely to have certain lion-like characteristics, such as a bold personality. Your daily horoscope or an astrologer will tell you what to expect or how to behave on any given day.

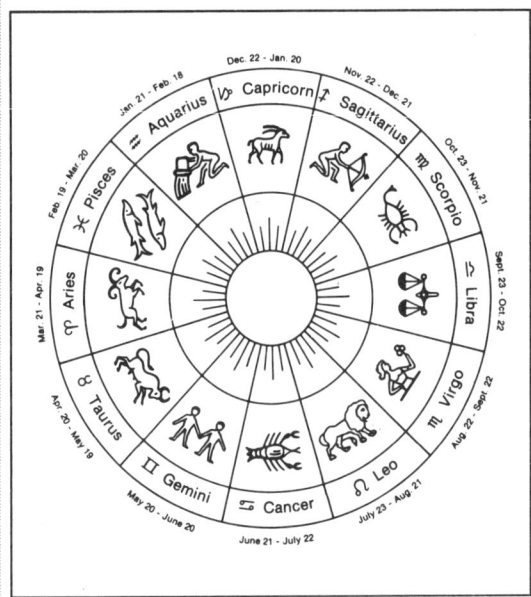

Signs of the Zodiac

Astrology, then, is the attempt to find life's meaning in the sky. It is based on the assumption that what happens in the sky affects what happens here on earth. Understanding astrology supposedly helps people to know how their lives have been influenced in the past and how they will be affected in the future by the heavenly bodies.

Problems with astrology

Astrology faces numerous scientific, practical, philosophical, and common-sense difficulties. Some of them are:

- Astrology is built on an ancient faulty view of the universe. It has an earth-centered view of the heavens, and new planets have been discovered since the birth of astrology.
- Because of shifts in the heavens, a person's birth-sign today is not what it would have been 2000-2500 years ago on the same date; yet astrology does not make this adjustment.
- Twins often have different futures, although according to astrology they should have similar fates.
- Astrology does not account for mass tragedies—such as airplane crashes, earthquakes, or the Jews and Christians killed under Hitler.
- Its predictions are often very vague. A *Time* magazine article some years ago (3/21/69) noted: "Break a leg when your astrologer told you the signs were good, and he can congratulate you on escaping what might have happened had the sign been bad. Conversely, if you go against the signs and nothing happens, the astrologer can insist that you were subconsciously careful because you were forewarned."
- Often astrological predictions fail to come true. For example, one study of more than 3000 public predictions by astrologers showed that only 11 percent were accurate.

Astrology in the Bible

In Old Testament times, pagan worship was often connected with astrology. The calf worship which crops up from time to time in Bible history involved the zodiacal sign Taurus, the bull. The well-known god Baal was the Phoenician sun-god, and the "Asherah pole" represented the worship of either Venus or the moon. She was the goddess of love, fertility, and good luck. Astrological worship involved such terrible practices as the sacrifice of children. (See 2 Kings 17:16-23.)

Through his prophets God warned: "Do not learn the ways of the nations or be terrified by signs in the sky, though the nations are terrified by them" (Jeremiah 10:2).

Nevertheless, throughout the years people have tried to reconcile astrology, at least in its milder forms, with the Bible. Luther's co-worker Philip Melanchthon advocated and practiced astrology, as do some Christians today who fail to see it for what it is.

In defense of this it's argued that the wise men who paid homage to the Christchild were astrologers and that God originally created the heavenly bodies as "signs." But the star of Bethlehem was a one-time supernatural phenomenon. God used it to lead the wise men to the newborn King, whom they properly worshiped. And in Genesis 1:14-19 we learn what kind of "signs" the heavenly bodies are. They "serve as signs to mark seasons and days and years." Our sense of time comes from these signs, but not our direction in life.

That comes from God. Though he doesn't tell us everything about the future, the Lord tells us what we need to know: "We know that in all things God works for the good of those who love him" (Romans 8:28). And so Jesus says, "Do not worry about tomorrow" (Matthew 6:34).

The brightest Star

In addition to being contrary to God's word, a danger of consulting the daily horoscope "for fun" lies in getting hooked on it. You may not take it seriously, but then one day the prediction for your sign comes true. You begin to wonder whether . . .

And although the daily horoscopes offer practical advice, there are many places to go for that. The best place, of course, is God's word. The book of Proverbs is full of advice for day-to-day living.

If we know people who are dabbling in astrology or deeply involved in it, we can point them in a better direction. We can point to Christ.

God loved us enough to give his only Son for our salvation; therefore, "how will he not also, along with him, graciously give us all things?" (Romans 8:32). Rather than entrusting our lives to the stars, then, we can entrust them to Jesus, "the bright Morning Star" (Revelation 22:16).

> **Fingertip facts:**
>
> *Founding:* Ancient Babylon.
> *Authority:* Advice and writings of astrologers.
> *Key teachings:* The future can be known.
> *View of the Bible:* Attempts to use some Bible passages to support astrology.
> *View of Jesus:* Not taken into account.
> *View of the Trinity:* Not taken into account.
> *Salvation:* The stars and planets hold our destiny.

Further reading:

Becker, Siegbert W. *Wizards That Peep: A Journey into the Occult.* Milwaukee: Northwestern, 1978.

Morey, Robert A. *Horoscopes and the Christian.* Minneapolis: Bethany House, 1981.

For study and discussion:

1. Many Scripture passages speak against astrology, especially in the Old Testament. Read 2 Kings 23:4-7. This passage relates the involvement of the southern kingdom, Judah, with the worship of idols and the stars. Where had the people been carrying out their astrological worship? What practices were connected with the worship? How did good King Josiah deal with it?

2. Read Isaiah 47:11-15. The Prophet Isaiah foretold the downfall of Babylon. With what other practices besides astrology

were the Babylonians involved? What is Isaiah's approach to the various superstitions, including astrology? Of what help would Babylon's astrologers be in the day of reckoning?

3. Read Psalm 19:1. According to this verse, what purpose do the heavens serve? How do they accomplish that purpose?

4. According to Deuteronomy 4:19, how are the heavens misused? How is this done in our day?

5. What differences are there between astrology today and the ancient astrology described in the Bible? What similarities are there? What practices are frequently associated with today's astrology?

6. There are more astrologers today than there have ever been in the history of mankind. In the U.S., astrology has seen a marked increase since the 1960s. To what factors might we attribute this growing interest?

7. It's been said that the person who believes in Jesus may not know what the future holds, but he knows who holds the future. How can worrying about the future and consulting astrologers show a lack of faith? What can we be sure the future holds? Why?

11.
Satanism

"*F*or our struggle is not against flesh and blood, but against the rulers, against the authorities, against the powers of this dark world and against the spiritual forces of evil in the heavenly realms" (Ephesians 6:12).

The prince of this world

This world is a spiritual battleground, in which God's people must struggle against the devil and his forces. So great is the devil's power that Jesus refers to him as "the prince of this world" (John 12:31).

From beginning to end, the Bible speaks of our enemy. Among his many names, he is referred to as *Satan,* a Hebrew word meaning enemy or adversary; *the devil,* that is, the slanderer or accuser; *Beelzebub,* Lord of the flies; *Belial,* worthlessness; *the tempter; the god of this world; the great dragon.* In whatever way God's word refers to him, it is clear he is real, a fallen angel. Not only are he and his demon followers real, but Satan is also powerful. No human beings can withstand him by their own power.

Satan's own churches

The great lie of Satan is that we can save ourselves. As he tempted our first parents in the Garden of Eden, so he tempts us to think we can safely go against God and his word. Those who are not living in the grace of God in Jesus Christ are living under the devil's dominion, whether they know it or not.

In our day, however, Satan has become so bold that he often dispenses with subtle temptations. He is openly worshiped. There are three recognized, legally protected satanist churches.

On April 30, 1966, the same year some theologians declared "God is dead," Anton LaVey founded the First Church of Satan. Ironically, LaVey does not believe in a real Satan. Rather, he sees the devil as symbolic of people's natural urge toward self-indulgence.

LaVey's *Satanic Bible* is a blasphemous attack on God and Christian doctrine. For example, he speaks of the "watery blood of your impotent mad redeemer," and refers to Christ crucified as "pallid incompetence hanging on a tree." The *Satanic Bible* is said to outsell the Bible two to one on college campuses.

Michael Aquino was a follower of LaVey who broke away and founded Temple Set, named after an ancient Egyptian god of evil. This group exalts mother nature and Nazi ideology.

The late 1970s saw Paul Valentine start what has been called the "most dangerous" of the satanic churches, the Church of Liberation. "Give me the young of today," boasts Valentine, "and I'll give you a satanic America tomorrow."

Many people practice Satanism aside from any organized "church." One researcher contends that the number of satanists in America rose from half a million in 1976 to a million and a half in 1985.

Devil worship

The so-called "black mass" goes back at least to seventeenth century Europe, where it was secretly practiced. It is a mockery of the Lord's Supper. The "altar" is a naked woman; the wine in the chalice is mixed with animal or human blood; the wafer is often laced with drugs; the crucifix is set upside down; the Scriptures are read backwards.

According to *Humane News,* animals are increasingly being abused, mutilated, and killed in satanic rituals. Small animals such as goats, cats, dogs, and chickens are prime targets. Some local humane societies won't put black cats up for adoption around Halloween. Much more terrifying are the reports of human sacrifice.

Satanists have their own "liturgical calendar" with special dates. Walpurgis Night, April 30, is "one of the greatest witches'

Sabbats" and "perhaps the most important date in the whole calendar of Satanism." Reportedly Adolf Hitler was heavily into the occult and took his own life on April 30, 1945, as a final, sacrificial tribute to the powers of darkness.

Certain symbols and words are standard

Symbols of Satan: the inverted pentagram and Baphomet, the scapegoat

among satanists. The inverted cross, lightning, the number 666 (or letter FFF), the occult pentagram, and the horned hand (index finger and little finger raised) are common satanic symbols. Satanists also use words spelled backwards: nema (amen), Natas (Satan), red rum (murder).

The tempter at work

In order to draw people, especially the young, more deeply into his grasp, Satan uses a number of "desensitizers." The game Dungeons and Dragons is one entrance into deeper involvement. Astrology—particularly when mixed with other methods of divining the future such as Tarot cards—can be another. Involvement in drugs and promiscuous sex play into Satan's hands.

Seemingly innocent forms of entertainment like some TV cartoons can condition youngsters for the real thing. One of the most commonly cited doors to deeper involvement is the Ouija board. People utilize it in an attempt to receive messages from the spirit world. A woman with whom I talked said she first entered into Satanism when she and friends at college experimented with this "game."

Heavy metal rock music is a frequent link to more blatant Satanism. Consider the name of one heavy metal group: Black Sabbath. Or consider just a few lyrics from the AC-DC album "Highway to Hell":

> Roaming through the endless wars
> Hold high his home we must
> Worried from the gates of hell
> In Lord Satan we trust.

Christians concerned about their friends and children should be aware of signs of involvement. These signs may include objects: collection of unusual books (on magic, paganism, rituals, Satanism), ritual items (candles, inverted crosses, oddly shaped knives), symbolic jewelry, drug use paraphernalia. Attitudes may also be symptomatic: obsession with heavy metal music, a new set of friends, more aggressive behavior, drop in school grades, interest in death, alienation from religion.

The great dragon defeated

In the preface to his famous *Screwtape Letters*, C. S. Lewis remarks, "There are two equal and opposite errors into which our race can fall about the devils. One is to disbelieve in their existence. The other is to believe, and to feel an excessive and unhealthy interest in them. They themselves are equally pleased by both errors, and hail a materialist or a magician with the same delight!"

Many in our high-tech society, including many churchgoers, scoff at the very idea of Satan. At the same time the devil and his influence become more and more brazen all around us.

Rather than panic, we can do something. If someone we know needs help we can try to direct that person to a Christian counselor or pastor. We can also pray.

Above all, we can share the word of the living God. He promises, "The one who is in you [Jesus] is greater than the one who is in the world [Satan]" (1 John 4:4). The woman mentioned before was delivered out of Satanism. How? Through Christians bringing her the word. She says, "Application and use of the word—there is no other way out."

Nor is there any other way to stay away from the devil in the first place. Read the Bible daily. When the devil tempted Jesus to worship him, our Lord replied, "Away from me, Satan! For it is written, 'Worship the Lord your God, and serve him only'" (Matthew 4:10). We need to know and be able to apply the word as Jesus did.

Christ has defeated the devil. "The reason the Son of God appeared was to destroy the devil's work" (1 John 3:8). Our Savior's perfect life, sacrificial death, and mighty resurrection belong to us by faith. His conquest of Satan and the powers of darkness is ours.

Stand firm. The victory is ours!

> **Fingertip facts:**
>
> *Founding:* 1966 by Anton Lavey as an organized church.
> *Authority:* Satanic Bible.
> *Key teachings:* Self-indulgence, opposition to everything Christian.
> *View of the Bible:* A book for weaklings.
> *View of Jesus:* Christ was but a man.
> *View of Trinity:* Unreasonable; to be rejected.
> *Salvation:* Freedom from all restraints.

Further reading:

Frederickson, Bruce G. *How to Respond to . . . Satanism* (part of the Concordia "Response Series"). St. Louis: Concordia, 1988.

Lewis, C. S. *The Screwtape Letters.* Old Tappan, NJ: Fleming H. Revell, 1978.

For study and discussion:

1. How can dabbling with such games as the Ouija board and Dungeons and Dragons lead to deeper involvement in the occult and perhaps even Satanism? Discuss also the influence of certain movies and some types of music.

2. What is the best prevention parents can give their children against the wiles of Satan? If they sense a child is getting caught up in satanic music or other practices, what might parents do?

3. Read Ephesians 6:10-18. This powerful passage describes "the full armor of God" in our battle against the devil. Note the various offensive and defensive weapons God furnishes in our spiritual warfare. Discuss how we are to use these mighty weapons.

4. Note the differences between (1) being drawn into Satanism and its practices and (2) being drawn away from God into apathy and indifference. In the end, how are both the same?

5. According to Anton LaVey, "The highest of all holidays in Satanism is the date of one's own birth, for we worship the individual and celebrate self-love." In what less blatant ways has this notion filtered through modern society? What does the Bible have to say about it? See 2 Timothy 3:1-5.

6. How does the establishment of organized satanic churches refute the popular notion that one church or religion is as good as another?

7. Consider the words from Martin Luther's great Reformation hymn, "A Mighty Fortress":

. . . .

The old evil Foe Now means deadly woe;
Deep guile and great might Are his dread arms in fight;
On earth is not his equal.

. . . .

This world's prince may still Scowl fierce as he will,
He can harm us none, He's judged; the deed is done;
One little word can fell him.

. . . .

What happens when we try to resist Satan by our own strength? On whose power must we rely? What victory has already been won? What end awaits "the accuser," that is, the devil? See Revelation 12:10-12; 20:7-12 ("Gog and Magog" represent the world's forces banded together against God's people).

12. Christ Crucified Is the Key

When we look at the vast array of non-Christian cults and religions, it's easy to become confused. Add to the older, established religions the hundreds of new ones that seem to spring up overnight and we face a bewildering forest of teachings, leaders, ideas, and practices. How can the Christian make sense of it all?

Happily, it's not necessary to know everything. A knowledge of basic teachings of several non-Christian religions makes it clear that certain common threads run through them all.

We need to be well-grounded in "the faith that was once for all entrusted to the saints" (Jude 3). Then the countless new doctrines pouring at us from every side will not easily sway us.

Other religions differ from the faith of Jesus Christ in a number of basic ways. We'll look at three.

1. Authority

All non-Christian faiths have an authority which to them is higher than the Bible. That authority may be considered God's

"We preach Christ crucified" (1 Corinthians 1:23).

own word, as Christian Scientists honor the writings of Mary Baker Eddy. Or it may be considered an aid to studying the Scriptures, such as the publications of the Jehovah's Witnesses. Although Witnesses would say that their teachings are not placed above the Bible, in reality they are.

Consider the sources of authority of the ten subjects of our study:

- Mormonism—the writings of Joseph Smith and pronouncements of the church hierarchy
- Jehovah's Witness—official Bible study aids of the organization
- Christian Science—the writings of Mary Baker Eddy
- Unification Church—writings of Sun Myung Moon
- Islam—the Quran
- Baha'ism—writings of Baha'i founders
- Hinduism—Hindu scriptures
- New Age Movement—the self
- Astrology—the movement of heavenly bodies as interpreted by astrologers
- Satanism—*Satanic Bible* and other blatantly anti-Christian sources.

Satanism openly defies the Bible. The Hindu Scriptures do not take it into account (although Hindu missionaries in the West express respect for it). The others all claim to honor the Bible as God's word. But such honor is mere lip service, as they deny one key Bible doctrine after another in favor of their own authority.

2. Salvation

Drawing upon their own authorities, all non-biblical faiths teach a way of salvation contrary to God's word. They may picture salvation in various ways, whether it be the Hindu *moksha* (union with the ultimate reality of Brahman) or the godlike state of the Mormons.

In whatever manner they portray salvation, they agree on the way to get there. Every religion except Christianity teaches that we must save ourselves.

Some may say that God makes salvation possible, or that Jesus showed the way, or that his death on the cross together with our good works brings salvation. But the Holy Scriptures teach that Jesus' sufferings and death are payment enough for the sins of all people.

We can add nothing to what Jesus has done for our eternal salvation. He died once and that one sacrifice was sufficient. This doctrine cannot be overemphasized.

The Bible clearly teaches it in many places. "But when this priest [Jesus] had offered for all time one sacrifice for sins, he sat down at the right hand of God" (Hebrews 10:12). This truth is taught throughout the Bible, Old Testament as well as New: "He was pierced for our transgressions, he was crushed for our iniquities; the punishment that brought us peace was upon him, and by his wounds we are healed" (Isaiah 53:5). And it is for this truth that the saints in heaven praise the Lamb of God: "You were slain and with your blood you purchased men for God from every tribe and language and people and nation" (Revelation 5:9).

Hand in hand with the unscriptural notion of earning our own salvation is a tendency to play down the seriousness of sin and its consequences. Rather than recognizing sin as a serious moral problem that keeps us from God and salvation, many see it as mere ignorance or a problem we can overcome with our own efforts.

3. Jesus

Every non-Christian religion has a distorted view of Jesus. Some, like the Mormons, will honor him as God. But they also teach that there are many other such gods and we can become one ourselves. To the Christian Scientist he is a divine idea. To the Jehovah's Witness he is a created angel. To the Muslim or

Baha'i he is a lesser prophet than Muhammed or Baha'u'llah. To Hindus he is another guru or one of many manifestations of God. To satanists he is a failure.

To the Bible-believing Christian, Jesus is the eternal Son of God—true God and true man. Far from being one among many religious leaders, Jesus is unique. He alone is God incarnate—that is, God in human flesh. He alone is Savior of the world. He alone has conquered sin, Satan, and death.

Sooner or later everyone must face Jesus' question, "What do you think about the Christ?" (Matthew 22:42). When discussing our faith with others, let us always focus on the person and work of Jesus Christ.

Sharing our faith

Someone has called the modern cults "the unpaid bills of the Christian church." For years much of Christendom has been in a state of sluggishness and decline. It has idly watched as false prophets have boldly pulled thousands—no, millions—of members out of the churches.

Our Lord calls on us to take up the struggle for the souls of men, women, and children. This means we need to know something about what's going on "out there." Make the effort to learn something about other religions.

More importantly, we need a deeper knowledge of the Bible itself. Regular church attendance is a must. So is regular home reading of the Scriptures. Make daily Bible reading your goal.

We need to apply the Scriptures. "When our Lord and Master Jesus Christ said, 'Repent,' he willed the entire life of believers to be one of repentance," wrote Martin Luther in the first of his Ninety-Five Theses. With the Lord's help let us turn from worldly ways and live a life of love.

God has given us the gift of prayer. Let's use it. Begin and end each day with prayer. Pray at meals, with fellow Christians, when alone. "Pray continually" (1 Thessalonians 5:17).

Finally, let's speak about our faith. As opportunity arises, tell others about Jesus. "But in your hearts set apart Christ as Lord," says the apostle Peter. And then, "with gentleness and respect," he urges us, "always be prepared to give an answer to everyone who asks you to give the reason for the hope that you have" (1 Peter 3:15,16).

> **Full circle**
>
> The following are excerpts from a woman who writes of how she came "full circle" back to her Lutheran-Christian faith:
>
> [Having lost my faith after leaving home] I was ripe for the Age of Aquarius movement, now known as the New Age movement. The teachings were easy for me to accept. I was god! . . . I got deeply into meditation, self-hypnosis, past-lives, special food diets . . . and all the rest of the spiritualism involved in their false teachings. I studied and practiced and eventually became a "Master Teacher" myself. As a result my life got worse.
>
> Terrible bouts of depression, a growing fear of the spirit world, and the prayers of family caused me to break completely with the cult's activities and associates.
>
> The next two years I prayed and prayed for faith in the true God. . . . Who was Jesus? Was Jesus the way to God? The gospel was difficult to believe; it seemed foolish, like a fairy tale. I couldn't believe in Jesus on my own. . . .
>
> It was an evening Lenten service in 1981; [the pastor's] sermon was entitled "Jesus the Exception to the Universal Law."
>
> Jesus is God! I finally understood! The Holy Spirit had opened my eyes and heart. It was wonderful, joyful, and so simple.
>
> I had come full circle. The Lord in his goodness had brought me back home.

Further reading:

Ehlke, Roland Cap. *Be Prepared to Answer*. Milwaukee: Northwestern, 1982.

Schuetze, Armin R. *Basic Doctrines of the Bible*. Milwaukee: Northwestern, 1986.

For study and discussion:

1. Review specific non-Christian cults and religions and how they differ with the Bible on basic issues. Especially note how in one way or another they all detract from the person of Je-

sus Christ. Why must all non-Christian groups in one way or another deal with Jesus? In the end, how will all people have to acknowledge him? See Philippians 2:6-11.

2. Because of the many religions confronting Christianity, what temptation might there be to dismiss doctrinal differences among Christian denominations? What would be wrong with this? See Matthew 28:19,20; Romans 16:17,18; 1 Timothy 1:3-6; 6:3-5.

3. In order not to lose members, what temptations might there be toward not carrying out church discipline in congregations? What does the Bible warn about allowing openly immoral life styles in Christian congregations? See 1 Corinthians 5.

4. Why is regular home Bible reading so important for Christians?

5. What assurances does God give that he will take care of his people no matter how troubled the times? See Psalm 46; Matthew 24:21-25; John 10:27-30.

6. What confidence and hope does a true account such as "Full circle" give as we confront today's many false religions and pray for those led into them?

7. The Bible records God's mighty hand in *history:* the Creation; his great deeds on behalf of his people (such as the Exodus); his prophecies of the Savior; the fulfillment of prophecy in the wonderful birth, life, death, and resurrection of Jesus Christ; the promise of his return at the end of the world. In addition to the historical nature of God's revelation, *two great doctrines*

run throughout the Bible: (1) mankind's sin and failure to keep God's law; (2) the good news of God's love and forgiveness in Christ. Discuss how the Bible's *historicity* and *law-gospel* focus make the Christian faith unique and priceless.